A JOURNEY OF RICHES

Building your Life from Rock Bottom

10 Inspiring stories that will lift your spirits

A Journey Of Riches - Building your Life from Rock Bottom
10 Inspiring stories that will lift your spirits © 2018
Spender, John

Copyright © 2018 John Spender
This work is copyright. Apart from any use as permitted under the Copyright Act 1968, no part may be reproduced, copied, scanned, stored in a retrieval system, recorded or transmitted, in any form or by any means, without the prior permission of the publisher.

The rights of John Spender to be identified as the primary author of this work has been asserted by him under the Copyright Amendment (Moral Rights) Act 2000 Disclaimer.

The author and publishers have used their best efforts in preparing this book and disclaim liability arising directly and indirectly, consequential or otherwise from its contents.

All reasonable efforts have been made to obtain necessary copyright permissions. Any omissions or errors are unintentional and will, if brought to the attention of the publishers, be corrected in future impressions and printings.

Published by Motion Media International
Editing: Chris Drabenstott, Gwendolyn Parker.
Cover Design: Motion Media International
Typesetting & Assembly: Motion Media International
Printing: Create Space

Creator: Spender, John - Primary Author
Title: *A Journey Of Riches - Building your Life from Rock Bottom*
10 Inspiring stories that will lift your spirits
ISBN: 978-0-6482845-3-6
Subjects: Self-Help, Motivation/Inspiration

Acknowledgements

Reading and writing is a gift that too few give to themselves, it is such a powerful way to reflect and gain closure from the past, reading and writing is a therapeutic process. The experience raises ones self-esteem, confidence and awareness of ones self.

I learned this when I created the first book in the '*A Journey Of Riches*' series, which is, now one of many books in the series with over 90 different co-authors from fourteen different countries. It's not easy to write about your own personal experience's and I honour and respect everyone of the authors who has collaborated in the series thus far. For many of the authors, English is their second language, which is a major achievement within its self.

In curating this anthology of short stories, I have felt such incredible joy, and I have been inspired by the amount of generosity, gratitude, and shared energy that this experience has given everyone.

The idea for this book came to me while I was interviewing Marion Hutton about her chapter in book seven *Making Empowering Choices,* we were chatting about the series and her career as a psychic medium. Out of no where she said *Building your Life from Rock Bottom,* would be a great title for the next book and three books later, here it is the tenth book in the series.

Of course, I could not have created this book without the nine other co-authors who each said YES when I asked them to share their insights into what Building your Life from Rock Bottom meant to them. Just like each chapter in this book makes for inspiring reading, each story represents one chapter in the life of each of the authors.

I'd like to thank all the authors for entrusting me with their unique memories, encounters and wisdom. Thank you for sharing and opening the door to your soul, so others may learn from your experience, may the readers gleam confidence from your success's and wisdom from your failures.

Thank you to my family, I know you are proud of me and how far I have come from that 10 year old boy who was just learning how to read and write at a basic level. Mom, Robert, Dad, Merril, my brother Adam and his daughter Krystal, my sister Hollie, her partner Brian and my nephew Charlie and my niece Heidi. Also my grandparents Gran n Pop who are alive and well and Ma and Pa who now resting in peace. They accept me just the way I am with all my travels and adventures around the world.

Thanks to all the team at MotionMediaInternational who have done an excellent job at editing and collating this book. It has been a pleasure working with you all on this successful project, and I thank you for your patience in dealing with the various changes and adjustments along the way.

Thank you, the reader for having the courage to look at your life and how you can improve your future in a fast and rapidly changing world.

And I'd enjoy to connect with readers, as I love sharing stories.

You can email me here: jrspender7@gmail.com

Thank you again to my fellow co-authors: Ryan Roth, Nicole Makin-Doherty, Suzie Martin Huening, Tom Baron, Kate Williams, Jen Valadez, Putu Cita, Christian Doherty, Jennifer Paul Pompei.

I hope you have enjoyed, this co-authored experience as much as I have. Love and light.

Praise

"If you are looking for an inspiring read to get you through any change, this is it!! This book is filled with many gripping perspectives, from a collection of successful international authors with a tonne of wisdom to share."

~ Theera Phetmalaigul, Entrepreneur/Investor.

"*A Journey Of Riches* is an empowering series that implements two simple words in overcoming life's struggles.

By diving into the meaning of the words "problem" and "challenge," you will find yourself motivated to believe in the triumph of perseverance. With many different authors from all around the world, coming together to share different stories of life's trials, you will find yourself drenched in encouragement to push through even the darkest of battles.

The stories are personal heart felt shares of moving through and transforming challenges into rich life experiences.

The book will move, touch and inspire your spirit to face and overcome any of life's adversities. A truly inspirational read. Thank you for being the kind open soul you are John!!"

~ Casey Plouffe, Seven Figure Network Marketer.

"A must read for anyone facing major changes or challenges in life right now. This book will give you the courage to move through any challenge with confidence, grace and ease."

~ Jo-Anne Irwin - Transformational Coach & Best Selling Author.

"I'm a fan of self-help books and I read them a lot. I love this book and the stories that are contained within them, but most of all I love the concept. I love that John Spender decided to do an anthology of stories from inspirational people. This is the type of book where you can either choose to be inspired by 10 different stories or choose a chapter that resonates with you the most.

As I read this book, it confirmed to me my life suspicion that things happen in our lives we can't control. It can be extremely devastating at times. It is those moments that bring us to our knees not knowing whether we can or even want to stand anymore. But, in these challenging moments, this book confirms to me that we do have one choice we can let go, make changes and embrace the new. It's the choice of how we decide to view these hardships. Our perspective determines what our life will be after these moments in our lives.

There were some very heart wrenching stories that were contained in these books. Some of them I even had to ask myself, "How do you even recover from a situation like that?"

Perspective. It all boils down to how we decide to view those hard challenges that come our way. At least that is what I took away from this book.

Thank you to John and his team of authors for getting together to create this book."

~ Kit Zakimi on Amazon.

"This next chapter in the *A Journey of Riches* book series will inspire and motivate you to move through any challenge or change in your life! This is a must read for anyone facing major challenges right now"

~ John Newman - Founder of MyRoadtoFinancialFreedom.com and Best Selling Author.

"A timely read as I'm facing a few changes right now. I liked the various insights from the different authors. This book will inspire you to move through any challenge or change that you are experiencing."

~ David Ostrand, Business Owner.

"I've known John Spender for a while now, I was blessed with an opportunity to be in book four in the series. I know that you will enjoy this new journey like the rest of the books in the series. The collection of stories will assist you with making changes, to deal with challenges and to see that transformation is possible for your life.

~Charlie O'shea, Entrepreneur.

"Amazing stories that remind us all that life presents us with challenges to bring out our best self. Thanks for the reminder. So inspiring and real."

~Jane Thorpe, Best Selling Author.

"Awesome! Truly inspirational! It is amazing what the human spirit can achieve and overcome! Highly recommended!!"

~Fabrice Beliard, Australian Business Coach and Best Selling Author.

"The *A Journey of Riches* book series is an inspirational read that will motivate you to take on any challenge in life. Make sure you grab your copy today."

~Katrina Gulabovski, Counsellor and Best Selling Author.

"The *A Journey of Riches* book series is a inspirational collection of books that will empower you to take on any challenge or change in life."

~Kay Newton, Midlife Stress Buster and Best Selling Author.

"*A Journey of Riches* book series are an inspiring collection of stories, sharing many different ideas and perspectives on how to overcome challenges, deal with change and to make empowering choices in your life. Open the book anywhere and let your mood chose where you need to read. Buy one of the books today, you'll be glad that you did! "

~Trish Rock, Modern Day Intuitive, Best selling Author, Speaker, Psychic & Holistic Coach.

"*Building your Life from Rock Bottom* is another inspiring read in the *A Journey of Riches* book series. The authors are from all over the world and each has a unique perspective to share, that will have you thinking differently about you're current circumstances in life. An inspiring read!"

~Alexandria Calamel, Success Coach and Best Selling Author.

"The *A Journey of Riches* books are a collection of real life stories, that are truly inspiring and give you the confidence that no matter what you are dealing with in your life, that there is a light at the end of the tunnel, and a very bright one at that.

Totally empowering!"

~ John Abbott, Freedom Entrepreneur.

"An amazing collection of true stories from individuals who have overcome great changes and who have transformed their lives and use their experience to uplift, inspire and support others."

~Carol Williams, Author-Speaker-Coach.

"You can empower yourself from the power within this book, that can help awaken the sleeping giant within you. John has a purpose in life to bring inspiring people together to share their wisdom, for the benefit of all who venture deep into this book *Building your Life from Rock Bottom*. If you are looking for inspiration to be someone special this book can be your guide."

~Bill Bilwani, Renown Melbourne Restaurateur.

"In *A Journey Of Riches: Building your Life from Rock Bottom*, the tenth book in the series, you will again catch the impulse to step up, reconsider and settle for only the very best for yourself and those around you. Penned from the heart and with an unflinching drive to make a difference for the good of all, *A Journey Of Riches* series is a must-read."

~Steve Coleman Author of *"Decisions, Decisions! How to Make the Right One Every Time."*

"If you want to be on top of your game? *A Journey of Riches* is a must read with breakthrough insights that will help you do just that!"

~ Christopher Chen, Entrepreneur.

"In *A Journey of Riches*, you will find the insight, resources and tools you need to transform your life. By reading the authors stories, you too can be inspired to achieve your greatest accomplishments and what is truly possible for you.

Reading this book activates your true potential for transforming, you're life way beyond what you think is possible. Read it and learn how you too can have a magical life."

~Elaine Mc Guinness, Best selling Author of *Unleash Your Authentic Self!*

"If you are looking for an inspiring read look no further than the *A Journey Of Riches* book series. The books are an inspiring collection of short stories, that will encourage you to embrace life even more. I highly recommend you read one of the books today!"

~Kara Dono, Doula, Healer and Best Selling Author.

"*A Journey of Riches* series is a must read for anyone seeking to enrich their own lives and gain wisdom through the wonderful stories of personal empowerment & triumphs over life's challenges. I've given several copies to my family, friends and clients to inspire and support them to step into their greatness. I highly recommend that you read these books, savoring the many aha's and tools you will discover inside."

~Michele Cempaka, Hypnotherapist, Shaman, Transformational Coach & Reiki Master.

"If you are looking for an inspirational read, look no further than the *A Journey Of Riches* book series. The books are an inspiring and educational collection of short stories from the authors soul itself, that will encourage you to embrace life even more. I've even given them to my clients too, so that they are inspired with their journeys in life, wealth, health and everything else in between.

I recommend you make it a priority, to read one of the books today!"

~Goro Gupta, Chief Education Officer, Mortgage Terminator, Property Mentor.

"The *A Journey Of Riches* book series is filled with real-life short stories of heartfelt tribulations turned into uplifting, self-transformation by the power of the human spirit to overcome adversity. The journeys captured in these books will encourage you to embrace life in a whole new way.

I highly recommend reading this inspiring anthology series."

~Chris Drabenstott, Best Selling Author and Editor.

There is so much motivational power in the *A Journey of Riches* series!! Each book is a compilation of inspiring, real-life stories by several different authors, which makes the journey feel more relatable and success more attainable. If you are looking for something to move you forward, you'll find it in one (or all) of these books.

~Cary Mac Arthur, Personal Empowerment Coach

I've been fortunate to write with John Spender and now call him a friend. *A Journey of Riches* book series features real stories that have inspired me and will inspire you. John has a passion for finding amazing people from all of the world, giving the series a global perspective on important subject matters.

~Mike Campbell, Fat Guy Diary, LLC

Table of Contents

Acknowledgements 3

Praise 6

Introduction 17

CHAPTER ONE
The Only Way Is Up
By John Spender 21

CHAPTER TWO
The Gift that Lies Within
Jen Valadez 40

CHAPTER THREE
Take Responsibility
By Ryan Roth 64

CHAPTER FOUR
Maintaining Resilience: Life after Rock Bottom
By Nicole Doherty 90

CHAPTER FIVE
When the Heart Hits Rock Bottom
By Tom Baron 114

CHAPTER SIX
Mastering Midlife
By Suzie Martin Huening 136

CHAPTER SEVEN
A Journey Home
By Christian Doherty 152

CHAPTER EIGHT
Shifting from Self-Pity to Self-Care
By Kate Williams 176

CHAPTER NINE
Hidden Shinning Jewel
By Putu Cita 196

CHAPTER TEN
The Power of Belief
By Jennifer Pompei 216

Author Autobiographies 234

Afterword 253

Introduction

I created this book and chose the different authors to share their personal insights, wisdom, and experiences to assist people who may be going through challenges, adversities, or changes similar to those of the authors.

Like all of us, each author has a unique story and insight to share with you. It just may be the case, that one or more of these authors have lived through an experience that is similar to circumstances in life right now and their words are the words you need to read to help you through it. Perhaps reading about one or more of these experiences will fill in the missing piece of your puzzle, so to speak, allowing you to move forward into the next phase on your journey.

Storytelling has been the way humankind has communicated ideas and learning throughout our civilization. While we have become more sophisticated, and life in the modern world is more convenient, there is still much discontent and dissatisfaction with one's reality. Many people have also moved away from reading books, and they are missing out on valuable information that can help them to move forward in life, with a positive outlook. I think it is important to turn off the T.V., to slow down, and to read, reflect, and take the time to appreciate everything you have in life.

I like anthology books because they carry many different perspectives and insights on a singular topic. I find that sometimes when I'm reading a book that has just one author I gain an understanding of their perspective and writing style very quickly and the reading becomes predicable. With this book and all of the books in the *A Journey of Riches* book series, you have many different writing styles and viewpoints that will help to shape you're own perspective with you're current set of circumstances.

Anthology books are also great because you can start from any chapter and gain a valuable insight or a nugget of wisdom without the feeling that you have missed something from the earlier chapters.

I love reading many different types of personal development books, because learning and personal growth is important to me. If you are not learning and growing, well, you're staying the same. Everything in the universe is growing, expanding, and changing. If we are not open to different ideas and different ways of thinking and being, then we can become close-minded.

The idea of this book series is to open you up to different ways of perceiving your reality, to give you hope, to give you encouragement, and to give you many avenues of thinking about the same subject. My wish for you, is to feel empowered to make a decision that will best suit you in moving forward with your life. As Albert Einstein said, "We cannot solve problems with the same level of thinking that created them."

With Einstein's words in mind, let your mood pick a chapter in the book and allow yourself to be guided to find the answers you seek.

"Rock bottom became
the solid foundation
on which I rebuilt
my life."

~ J.K. Rowling

CHAPTER ONE

The Only Way Is Up

By John Spender

"The darkest cave that you are most afraid of facing holds your greatest treasure."

~ Joseph Campbell

Seek Your Treasure

This chapter is for anyone that has the courage to expand into life and face all aspects of yourself in the quest to live to your highest potential and risk the fact that you may never get there. Warning: this chapter maybe dangerous because it will mean looking at your addictions, your shame, your fears, your guilt, and anything else that you avoid and that makes you feel uncomfortable. Why would I write a chapter like this? Well, believe it or not, your stressings are your blessings. Your pain is the gift in your life; the very thing you are avoiding is the thing that will set you free. If you are seeking your own internal treasure, read on.

Knowing the questions for the life you wish to live will give you the answers that you seek. Some questions that I feel everyone needs to face, or will be faced with at one point in time, are questions like, what makes me happy? What is my purpose? How can I create the life of my dreams? What type of person will make me happy? And the list can go on and on. Are these the best questions to ask ourselves when we are seeking answers and solutions because something is seemingly missing from our lives? Surely to ask any question is better than shelving all curiosity about improving our circumstances and quality of life.

What about questions such as, what am I most afraid of in my life? Public speaking? Death? Travel? The unknown? Being seen? Allowing love in my life? Being in a relationship?

Maybe you're most afraid of your greatness or to be seen as a failure or to feel or express vulnerability.

To not want more from life is to risk being the frog in the slowly boiling water, simmering away and not realizing that you are slowly boiling to death. To want more out of life is to face and chose your adversity. If you don't, life will create it for you. Seeking safety just might be the most dangerous and risky thing that you can chose to do. So, what is the answer to discovering the treasure you seek? Could it be as simple as finding a vision or passion and taking consistent action until it is realized and then repeating? Or maybe it is living a balance between all your activities and responsibilities that bring you joy and happiness.

Is your treasure being content and happy with what you have and simply enjoying the process that we call life?

Let's not get stuck in the endless questions, both negative and positive, only to forget that life is to be experienced and that we have the power to change direction, delete a scene, and create a new one in any given moment, and that means facing all aspects of our lives including exploring the places that we fear the most.

What Is Rock Bottom?

Most topics of conversation are debatable, and most debates are irrelevant to the solution. Continuous and consistent action is the real equalizer in this world and it is our differences that makes the difference towards solving any challenge, problem, or issue. Naturally, rock bottom is going to be different for each person. One person's rock bottom will be seen as an adventure or an opportunity by another person. That is the power of perspective and the meaning that we give to our experience. Are you giving your experience a disempowering meaning or an empowering definition? and how can you tell which is which? The answer is gauged simply by the way you feel about your experience in any given moment.

Let's start with what would be your rock bottom. The answer lies in all aspects of your life that you are constantly trying to protect and maintain. It's really anything that you would consider anything that could turn your world upside down and completely break your routine of living and being. Would shatter your expectations of how your life should be. Your sense of security, belonging, and self-worth, and to take all these things away from you, that's your rock bottom. Escaping from the reality of these things can also create your rock bottom, either through addictions to food, drugs, sex, or anything else that doesn't serve you. Take away a person's home, earning capacity, confidence, ability to provide value for humanity, and/or to take away the belief that there is a solution to your challenges, and you have a rock-bottom moment. At the end of the day, your rock bottom will be whatever you decide it to be, right? Knowing your rock bottom will enable you to know what you don't want and will give you the character and strength to explore and create the life that you do want. So, why are we so afraid to experience low points in our lives?

At some point in your life, you're going to go through a moment that you wouldn't wish on your worst enemy, the moment that you would consider your rock bottom. While seeing this as a nightmare will create a nightmare, seeing rock bottom as an adventure will create an adventure.

Whatever you believe, know, and defend will become your reality. Sometimes that reality becomes a friend that we know as depression. This concept of depression being a friend is one I learned from Rod E Hairston when I interviewed him for the book we collaborated on called *A Journey of Riches: Transformation Calling*. With this idea, he inspired the following awaking in me.

The concept, as I understand it, is this: that depression is a friend we build up. We build this friend up to be something more than it really is and, at the core of this friend that doesn't serve us is the fact that he is just energy. To those who experience depression, it's their most comfortable, reliable friend and, in a way, creating this friend becomes an addiction, a presence that they can neither live with nor without. The friendship will continue until you decide to give up the need for this particular friend in your life and transform that friendship, or energy, in the most loving and peaceful way. The trick is to see it for what it is—energy—and if you are doing depression, it means you have big energy and you can transmute that heavy energy into its opposite and begin to create joy and happiness and to add value to your world. To break its hold on you really can be as simple as changing the meaning you give to depression.

Depression is staying at rock bottom for way too long, and we need to continually break its hold on us. One way is to change the meaning we give to it. Another is to break the pattern by going for a walk or doing something that we love to do. My friend, depression, doesn't come around as often as he used to since I developed a strong personal development game plan. He still visits every now and then, but he doesn't stay for long. We did have a rock-solid friendship for about five years, until I began traveling and focusing my energy on other friends, like happiness and joy. As you can imagine, my life has dramatically changed in a positive and bright way!

Rock Bottom Is an Opportunity

It was late at night when I creeped up the driveway of my old apartment. The sound of the crashing waves below muffled my footsteps. I placed the key into the side door and my cat, Lucky, was waiting for me silently in the garage to the apartment I could no longer afford to pay the rent for. I had reached a low point in my life, such that I hadn't experienced for ten years or more.

I was no longer able to pay my bills and flourish like I had once done when running my landscape business. The good news was that it wasn't a result of using drugs or associating with the wrong crowd, like my previous rock-bottom experience had been. Have you ever wanted to pursue a lofty dream and work in your ideal career? Well, I had sold my successful landscape gardening business only nine months earlier to become a life coach. I had stopped drinking heavily and quit my recreational drug-taking. When you want to make a career change, you invest in your education, learn the skills in your new vocation, and you put them to work. I did just that, investing in a solid year-long coaching program before I sold my business. But here I was unrolling my sleeping bag on a piece of cardboard in the middle of winter. At least I had Lucky to snuggle with.

How did this all happen? And, more importantly, how was I going to get out of this mess?

Once evicted, I gave most of my belongings away, and I put the rest in the back of my pickup. A friend let me stay at his place for five days, but no longer than that, as he was afraid I was going to sponge off him. In the beginning of my coaching practice, things were looking good. I was on contract, coaching for a large seminar company in Australia, traveling around the country, coaching people about having a successful mind-set. I was volunteering my time at Mission Australia once a week, teaching NLP (Neuro Linguistic Programming) to the borderline homeless. I was also attracting a few private clients as well, and I had a professional-looking website with great testimonials.

Looking back in reflection at this rock-bottom moment, I was 30 grand in debt (from paying for all the trainings), no consistent income, and no home in the middle of winter. I now see that it would have been wiser to have kept my landscape gardening business, at least the garden maintenance side of things. This would have given me a steady income stream while I pursued the new endeavors of coaching, speaking, and writing. I could have also moved into an apartment that was more affordable. And rather than attending a personal development seminar every weekend and flying overseas to do many trainings as well, it may have been more sensible to focus on one or two trainings. I sold the business to my manager, took on the coaching full-time, and invested in speaking and writing trainings around the world. To learn one new skillset in a completely different field is challenging, but to learn three completely new skillsets and to run a new business was too much for me to handle.

Also, when you are working with people to support them in solving their challenges, I feel it's best to be coming from a place of total support without the express need to work with a particular person. When you come from a place of need to help a client because you have to pay your bills, it creates an unconscious needy energy that unconsciously repels the potential clients. At least that's what I experienced. This was after investing about 90 grand USD in trainings around the world. They were great trainings from some of the top people in personal development, but, in hindsight, I felt that I took on too much too quickly and I didn't give myself time to integrate what I was learning in my own life. And it's kind of how I managed my friendship with depression, by making myself so busy that I wouldn't have time to entertain my friendship with him.

Here I was looking for employment. All of my coaching clients for various reasons had finished working with me. It was a humbling experience to look for employment again after being self-employed for the past five years. I found casual work straight away. I just had enough money to cover my expenses and to feed myself and my cat, and I slept in the garage for a week. Lucky's cat food was quite cheap, and I lived on tins of baked beans, tuna, tomatoes, and bread. During the day, I used to leave Lucky in the local cemetery, and I'd come and get him after work. He didn't like staying there at all, and when I returned to get him, he used to look at me like, "Why on earth are you leaving me here?" When I received my first pay, I moved into a share house in Bondi, and I was thankful that my new flatmates allowed me to keep Lucky. Even though it was a short-term lease, it was a step up from the garage floor.

 After a few casual jobs and share houses, I eventually secured a well-paid contract running the company's maintenance division and bringing in new business through BNI (Business Networking International). I moved into a beautiful share house, five houses from the ocean, and I started coaching again, all in three long, challenging months. I even ran my first speaking event at the end of the year with 26 people attending and, though I didn't bring any new coaching clients on board from the seminar, it was a positive step in the right direction. I kept reading personal development books and listening to audios of my favorite speakers like Dr. Wayne Dyer, Dr. John Demartini, and Hay House Radio. This allowed me to stay positive and maintain resourceful states of mind. I had a good group of friends, and we used to meet up in each other's lounge rooms to practice our public speaking skills and try out new content. I became a member of two Toastmasters clubs, and I entered all the public speaking contests that they had. I continued to run small events. I was writing a book, and my confidence began to grow.

During this time, I kept my expenses low and ate all my meals at home. So, when I finally began to generate a healthy income again, I treated myself and feasted at my favorite sushi bar in Bondi Junction, *Sushi Express*. I ordered all my favorites, the glistening and succulent salmon sashimi, the barbeque eel with that delicious sauce, the healthy sea weed sushi, all their various kinds of salmon sushi, and the egg boat is, like, wow! And I hear myself say wow every time I eat it. Instead of the seaweed roll, they use a flatten cooked egg yolk that is soft, wrapping the rice and thinly sliced avocado with fish roe. It's a cornucopia of flavors in every bite. I spent about 60 bucks, but it was absolutely worth it, especially after I had been so disciplined saving my money and clearing my debts.

When you find yourself in a challenging situation, you need to focus on the light, the positives in your environment, and walk towards your desired life.

Make Rock Bottom An Adventure

I remember when I used to sit on the cliff tops watching the waves crashing onto the rocks below with Lucky by my side, and I would feel the feelings of being given an amazing opportunity doing what I loved. I was quite general. I didn't even know what that looked like, but the feelings of an eminent positive experience were strong. Sure enough, an amazing opportunity came my way. After 12 months of grinding away and showing up day in and day out, an opportunity presented itself to me. Just before I'd become homeless, I had been trying out for a trainer's position for a large seminar company to run some of their NLP trainings, and I had missed my chance to work with them. I flew all the way to Las Vegas, only to miss out in favor of another person. A year later, the founder had a falling out with his business partner and was moving to Asia to start a new training company, running NLP trainings in Singapore and Bali.

The offer was to move to Bali with accommodations and living expenses paid for, and I would help grow the business. There would be no pay for the first three months, and I would need to pay for my own airfare. I felt excited by the opportunity; I knew that it would be a good chance for me to grow as a person. Still, I had to ponder the decision, because the only times that I had worked for free was when I was volunteering for Drug Arm and Mission Australia. I found an astrologer online and I gave her my place of birth, time, and date. Three days later, I received an amazing report. One of the many insightful pieces of wisdom she offered was that I would be faced with an unusual opportunity, either now or in the future, and, no matter what, I had to say yes! The woman was emphatic about this, and she said it would be an overseas opportunity where I would be helping many people from around the world. I was amazed at the accuracy of the information that she provided.

I knew I had to take this opportunity and, although it was without pay, supporting people was one of my highest values. I arrived at the airport in the late afternoon and no one was there to pick me up. The team was at an event in Singapore, and they wouldn't return for another two days. They had forgotten to tell the driver. I was surprised, but I thought, *No biggie. I've been to Bali before. I'm sure I can work this out.* They were staying at Dragonfly in Ubud, I would hire a driver to take me there.

The problem was, the driver had no idea where it was. Again, no biggie. I would ask Google Maps, but it wasn't listed, nor did they have a website. It turns out that they had only just opened. I had the driver that I'd hired to drop me in the middle of town, and I planned to ask some of the locals where this place was. Everyone that I asked had no idea where this Dragonfly place was located, and I began to feel annoyed. Right in the moment of frustration, I saw a beautiful lotus flower and I decided to take a photo. I placed my bag on the ground, took my camera out, and, just as I was taking the photo, I felt a stinging sensation on my foot and I dropped my camera into the drain.

Now I was feeling completely irritated with these tiny fire ants biting my feet, which was surprisingly painful. Luckily, my camera was waterproof, and a few people came out to assist me. One person had a flashlight on his phone, and so I could see my camera. Another two people came over, one with a towel and the other with moist napkins, and they helped me to lower myself into this drain to retrieve my camera, and then helped me to clean myself up and to wipe away the ants.

The sense of gratitude that I was experiencing was immense. It was no surprise that the next person I asked knew where Dragonfly was and agreed to take me part of the way with his car. However, I would need to walk the rest of the way, as the retreat center was in the middle of the rice fields. You either had to walk or find someone with a motorbike to take you there. The driver found the number to the place through his friend, and they sent two of their staff on motorbikes to bring me and my bags to the accommodation. To say that the path to Dragonfly was narrow was an understatement. Wow! What an adventure! The accommodation was beautiful. It had a wet edge swimming pool overlooking the rice fields, with fish ponds and gardens as the border to pathways leading to quaint timber bungalows. My room was actually a dorm with bunk beds. Oh, no! I thought back to my childhood years when I use to share a room with my older brother. This time I made sure I had the bottom bunk, and I laughed out loud to myself.

That first week was interesting indeed. By the end of the week we were a team of eight, including the founder. Our first full team meeting was a real eye-opener into the lack of financial resources and how much had to be done to make this business a success. We were basically starting from scratch, and we needed to hit the ground running in terms of generating sales. They already had a deal with promoters in Singapore, and the founder had sold his NLP event from the stage with a little bit of success.

At night when we went to bed, we would be awakened early in the morning, either by roosters (the Balinese love to bet on rooster fights) or the founder, who had hooked up with one of the team and her screams of pleasure echoed throughout the whole place. But this wasn't as bad as the homemade wind chimes that were used to scare the birds out of the rice paddies. The noise was deafening. On various mornings, one of the team would run through the rice field and pull out the chimes. After doing this, that team member would be covered in mud up to his/her knees, but the silence made it worthwhile and eventually the farmers used nets instead. My experience of moving to Bali showed me that adversity can be an adventure to live, and although we faced many challenges, it was like an exciting roller coaster ride. To others in the team, they saw the experience as their worst nightmare and only lasted a month. It really is a matter of perspective.

Rock Bottom Is a Launch Pad to Success

Robert Downy Jr is one of the highest paid actors today in Hollywood, and he has won many prestigious awards and accolades as an actor, including being nominated for an Academy Award for Best Actor for his performance in Chaplin (1992). He was a child actor, appearing in his first film at the age of five. His dad was an underground movie director in the sixties and recreational drug-taking was considered normal in his circle. It's believed that Downy Jr's dad gave him his first joint at a very young age. His neighborhood in New York was artistic, and he lived in a hippy community.

He eventually moved to Hollywood with his dad after his parents were divorced. He dropped out of high school and was landing roles in many films and was considered a talented actor by movie critics. He was building a strong fan base while simultaneously indulging in recreational drug-taking, and it's reported that bonding time with his father also included drug consumption. His recreational drug habit spiralled out of control after playing the lead role in *Less than Zero* (1987). His character for this movie was an out-of-his-mind drug abuser, an exaggerated version of himself at the time. A few years later, his life was at rock bottom and his addiction to drugs raised its ugly head in a big way.

In early 1996, Downey Jr was caught speeding on Sunset Boulevard, howling at the moon like a dog while in the possession of heroin, cocaine, and an unloaded .357 Magnum handgun. He was released without being charged, and only two weeks later his neighbors found him in their young daughter's bed sleeping. They tried to wake him up, but he was intoxicated with copious amounts of drugs and alcohol. The police were called, and his arrest became very public. It seemed that for about five years he was in the limelight for the wrong reasons.

In 2001, while on parole, Robert was found barefoot, wandering around Culver City, which at that point in time was a derelict part of L.A., and he was arrested on suspicion of being under the influence of drugs and alcohol. He was later fired from his role on the hit TV show *Ally McBeal*. He became the actor no one wanted to hire. The out-of-work Downy Jr was sent to a drug and alcohol rehabilitation center. This was after he was sentenced for three years to a California substance abuse treatment facility and a state prison in Corcoran, California. He stayed there for less than a year. Downey was surprisingly freed when a judge ruled that his collective time in correctional facilities (from 1996 - 1999 arrests) had earned him an early reprieve.

His life turned around when his friend and fellow actor, Mel Gibson, recommended him for a role in the film *Gothika* (2003) starring alongside Halle Berry. And this is the film where he met his now-wife, Susan Levin, a producer. They were married in 2005, and they are still married to this day. Downy Jr credits his comeback success to Susan's influence. He has since starred in *Iron Man* (2008), *Avengers* (2012), and *Captain American* (2016), to name a few. That's some turn around, especially when it looked like he would never act again. Through drugs, prison, and rehab, Downy Jr has bounced back in a big way. He is now worth more than $250 million, happily married, and still acting to this day.

When you are experiencing rock bottom, when your circumstances seem hopeless, it is so easy to stay there and feel sorry for yourself. It's a test of your character if you can rally and rebuild your life. You may be going through a rock-bottom moment right now, and I hope this chapter has inspired you to make positive changes in your life, to reframe the meaning you give to low points in your life and to see your low points from a different perspective. Rock bottom doesn't have to be a place where you stay. It can be a launch pad for bigger and better things to come. First you need to decide that things are going to be different. Once you decide, it becomes much easier to turn things around. And who knows? Your resourcefulness just may be the inner treasure you have been seeking.

You careful that you aren't stuck living the same old lie day in day out everyday, for the rest of your life.

Above everything else, seek adventures.

"Sometimes, you have
to get knocked down
lower than you have
ever been to stand
back up taller than
you ever were."

~ Unknown

CHAPTER TWO

The Gift that Lies Within

Jen Valadez

As I sit down preparing to write this chapter, I start by taking a few deep breaths and connect with my Higher Self. It is within the stillness and silence that these words begin to flow through me, and I know that I am being guided.

The stillness is where all the answers reside. Your breath is the vehicle that connects to you the Oneness that you are. You have the ability to transcend all fears, all limitations, all blocks, all suffering. Come back to your breath and connect with me.

Through the stillness of your breath, all words will flow from you, and you will know what needs to be spoken. Trust the process, connect daily, and it will be written. Your words will inspire many, and you will know the essence of who you truly are.

I am here always and in All Ways. I am the music that inspires you. I am in the flavor and aroma of your morning cup of coffee. I am in the smiles you receive from clients and strangers throughout the day. I am the embrace of Lon's arms wrapped around you, reminding you of how loved you are. I am in your kids' smiles, their sense of humor, and in their eyes. Your soul and their soul are One. There is no separation from me. All that is in this human experience exists as one vast open space. We are One.

Be still, be present, and you will know me within every experience of your life. I am here always and within All Ways.

I grew up the youngest of four kids in the small town of Orem, Utah. I was raised as a Mormon. We were taught that everyone who belonged to our church had the opportunity to make it into the highest kingdom of heaven if they lived an honest, clean life and repented for all of their sins. We were also taught that our church was the only true church on the earth and those who didn't belong to our church would not make it into the highest kingdom of heaven. We were God's chosen people and it was our job to spread the gospel to as many people as possible, so that they may have the same opportunity to make it into heaven and be saved.

Missionary work and baptisms for the dead were an important part of helping others to become members of our church. No, we didn't actually baptize dead people; we would stand in proxy for someone who had died and go through the baptism ceremony for them. I remember as a little girl, many concepts within our church were very confusing to me. My aunt didn't belong to our church, but in my eyes she was a very good, loving person. How could God not allow her into the highest kingdom of heaven? We were taught never to question our faith, or the leaders of our church. We must "follow the prophet, don't go astray. Follow the prophet, he knows the way." Those were the words to a popular children's hymn in our church. If we were to question the teachings of our church, this was considered to be Satan using his powers on us to make us stray from the truth. We were also taught however, to study and pray in order to gain a testimony of the truth. Even at a very young age, these two teachings seemed to contradict each other. Study and pray to gain a testimony of the truth, but make sure your truth fits into the structure and guidelines of our church. What if my testimony didn't fit into the structure of the church? I had so many questions as a young child, but no voice to express how I was feeling. At the age of eight, we had the opportunity of being baptized to become a member of the church. Although we were taught that this was something we were to pray about and decide if we were ready for, no eight-year-old really went through this process. If we were to actually decide not to baptized at this age, this decision would cause a lot of heartache, sadness and remorse for the entire family. Baptism wasn't a choice; it was something you just did because you were told it was the right thing to do. I remember my baptism day being a very confusing and conflicting day for me. I didn't want to be baptized, but felt as though I had no other choice. I didn't want to disappoint my family.

From as young as I can remember up until the age of 12, I was sexually abused by my grandfather. My grandparents lived not far from my home and they would often babysit me. I remember my grandfather would always give my grandmother a list of items to pick up at the grocery store, and when she left the house, this is when the abuse would occur. My grandfather told me that I had a very serious disease and that what he was doing to me was helping to cure the disease. He told me to never tell anyone about the disease, because if I did, they would catch the disease and die. I grew up believing I was dying, although internally, I felt fine. The fear of having a disease caused me to be very shy and timid. I didn't feel like I could get close to anyone or tell anyone what I was going through. I didn't want anyone to die from the disease I had. I felt very scared and alone, and learned at a very young age that I was on my own. There was no one I could talk to or lean on for strength but myself. I worried constantly that someone would find out.

School was very hard for me. I struggled to make friends, and I worried constantly. I cried on a daily basis, and the school secretary would often call my mother to come pick me up. My mother seemed very exhausted with this daily routine of picking me up halfway through the day, and I remember one day begging her to be a "stay at home" mom. I remember her saying, "Jenny you worry too much", and that she needed to get back to work, and would be taking me to my grandparents' home. She told me that she was sorry she couldn't stay home with me, but I would be fine with my grandparents until she could get off work. I was so angry at myself that day! I didn't understand why I couldn't just be normal and stay at school like all the other kids. I wanted to feel safe and secure in my own home with my Mom. I longed for this connection with her.

At the age of 12, my father received the news that his job was being transferred to St. George. At this time, my older brother and sisters were all moving into adulthood and starting their lives. I would be the only one moving to St. George with my parents. The thought of moving somewhere new was very scary, but at the same time, I understood this to be a new beginning. The abuse would soon be over. I remember the day so clearly in my mind, driving away from Orem, I knew I was finally free. I cried the entire way to St. George, as my parents tried to reassure me that everything would be okay. I would meet new friends and would still be able to see my brother and sisters often. My parents had no idea that I was crying tears of relief and a new found freedom. During the trip to St. George, a very peaceful feeling washed over me. I was overwhelmed with an understanding of clearly knowing within that I was not dying, and I made a promise to myself that day to never think about what happened to me in Orem ever again.

Moving to St. George was the best thing that could have happened to me. I made new friends and slowly started to come out of my shell. The worry and fear slowly faded with time and I soon forgot about what had happened to me. It was as though I completely blocked my childhood from memory. I became very passionate about dancing, ballet in particular. Dancing became a very creative outlet for me and I felt as though I could express myself freely. When I danced, I felt connected to something bigger than myself, and I dreamt of one day moving to New York City and becoming a professional ballerina.

When I was about 16 years old, I woke up one morning from a bad dream. I had dreamt that I was being abused by my grandfather. This dream began happening more and more until one morning I realized this was something that had really happened! Slowly all of the details started flooding back into my memory, and I felt that familiar sick feeling of worry, shame, and guilt that I had felt as a little girl. I was guided by something internal to start writing these memories down in my journal as a means to help me release it from my body. With time, I stopped having these bad dreams and my journal was put up high on a shelf in my bedroom. I continued on with my life, always feeling as though I had a dark secret I was keeping from the world.

I fell in love with James during my senior year of High School. He was different from all the other boys at school. He drove a motorcycle, and wore bright blue Dr. Marten boots that had orange flames running up the sides of them. He also carried his wallet attached to a chain that ran down the side of his hip and back up to his belt buckle. He was pretty "bad ass", and carried himself with such confidence. He was definitely NOT the type of boy my parents wanted me to date, which pretty much made him perfect in my eyes. At this point in my life, I had started to become more and more rebellious and began pushing back at the boundaries my parents and religion had set for me. My dad was the bishop of our church during this time, and I was out to prove to the world that I wasn't the good little church-goer my parents wanted me to be. Partying and drinking became a way for me to escape all the pain that was going on internally. I wanted to spend every minute with James. We ditched school together quite often and would find ways to sneak out on the weekends to camp out under the stars together. I felt safe, content, and happy in his arms. I could be myself around him, and I dreamt of the day we would get married and start a family. As high school came to an end, we began to slowly grow apart and both felt the need to create space in our relationship. I moved into an apartment downtown with some roommates and tried to settle into college life. Three weeks into school I discovered I was pregnant. I called James in tears, and he picked me up to go for a ride. "Well, I guess we're getting married," were the first words he said to me. It was very clear that this was not what he wanted, but what he felt forced to do. I wanted desperately to marry him, but after hearing these words, I knew the feeling wasn't mutual. I didn't want James to marry me because I was pregnant, I wanted him to marry me because he loved me.

We decided to talk to both of our parents and let them know what we were facing. We were met with shock, anger and disapproval and told we needed to get married or give the baby up for adoption. The second choice wasn't an option for me. Within this very short period of time, I had already fallen in love with the new life growing inside of me. My parents were truly devastated with the news and I felt like, once again, I had fallen short of their love and approval. Getting pregnant out of wedlock was considered a big sin in our religion, and I felt I had embarrassed my entire family. Within the next few days, it was decided that we would get married, and plans for a small wedding started to slowly come together. During this time, James became more and more distant. I tried to ignore the way he was treating me and focus on the wedding plans, but deep inside I knew this wasn't what he wanted. Three days before the wedding, James had disappeared with friends and I had a sinking feeling that this is how our marriage would always be. In that moment I knew I couldn't marry James. My heart had never been so broken. I felt as though my world was crumbling down around me and I had no idea how to save it. My dreams of living happily ever after were gone in an instant.

The next few months were very difficult, as depression, worry, and morning sickness began to take over my body. Living back at home with my parents was a huge blow to my pride. I worried constantly about how I was going to provide for this baby all alone. These days were some of the most lonely, depressing days I had ever felt.

My father's secretary knew a young man who had just recently returned home from a mission, and she insisted that we meet. I had absolutely no desire to start dating someone new. I was grieving the loss of James, and preparing to raise a baby alone. After much arguing and convincing, I finally decided to go on a blind date with Ken, the return missionary. Our first date was extremely awkward. I was four months pregnant at the time, and felt very self conscious and out of place. Ken was a very nice man. Perfect in every way if you asked my parents. He was an active member of our church, and ready and quite willing to take on the responsibility of a young pregnant bride. I believed at the time that Ken was the only man that would ever accept me and my baby, and he was also a way of winning back the approval of my parents and family. I was beginning to think that maybe it was time to start giving the church a real chance. My life obviously wasn't going the way I had dreamt it would go. Maybe this was God's way of punishing me for all of my sins.

One evening after coming home from a date with Ken, I found my mother and father in the kitchen. They both looked at me as my mother was crying and told me we needed to talk. My Mother had found my journal and had read the horrible things my grandfather had done to me. She looked completely distraught as they began to inform me that the abuse had also happened to my two older sisters. I just stood there in complete shock. I couldn't believe what they were telling me. How could this happen? How could he do this to all of us? And how could they allow him to babysit me if they knew he had done this to my sisters? I was completely horrified and enraged. I had never felt so betrayed in all my life. I had lived with this secret all my life, and they knew about it the entire time. They told me they didn't know that he was abusing me, that my grandfather had told them he had repented of his sins and they believed he was telling the truth.

My grandfather was dying during this time, and I hadn't seen him since I had moved to St. George. My father felt it was important for all of us to bring closure to the situation before he passed away. We made plans to travel to Orem to see him, give him a chance to apologize for what he had done, and make peace before saying goodbye. I was on my way to Orem when my grandfather passed away. I was so relieved to hear of his passing. I wasn't ready to see him, or make peace with what he had done. I was still raging internally, and not ready to let go of the past. Attending his funeral was extremely difficult as I pretended to mourn the loss of a man that had completely stolen my childhood from me. I felt an emptiness within, as if I'd been completely defeated by a power much bigger than myself. I remember standing there, a shell of a person, feeling so small and worthless with tears running down my face as our family and friends reminisced about this mans life. I felt the little girl within me die right along with him. I would never get that part of my life back, and now I was getting ready to bring a new life into the world. How had this happened? This wasn't the life I had chosen to live.

A few months later Ken and I were married by my father. I remember walking down the aisle, looking at Ken and thinking, I have no idea who this person is that I'm about to marry. There is no way out, this was my life now. Two months later, I gave birth to Tanner at only 18 years old.

Tanner brought so much love and light into my world. He was my reason for getting out of bed in the morning. He was my everything, my entire world, the one thing that could instantly put a smile on my face and make all the pain disappear for a moment. Although I struggled with depression, Tanner gave me something to stay focused on, and I began to settle into this new routine of being a wife and mother.

The conflict and fighting within my marriage started a week after our honeymoon. In the beginning, I was often scared of Ken, as he would enforce his dominance and control over me. He wasn't physically abusive, but I knew if I were to push back, it could easily turn that way. There was never any question who was in charge. I felt as though I walked on eggshells constantly, and was always trying to keep the peace. Many things went left unsaid, as I still felt as though I had no voice. I was going through all the motions, smiling when needed, allowing others to believe all was well in my world, while feeling completely empty inside.

A few days after Tanner's first birthday, I found out that I was pregnant again. I worried that there would be no possible way that I could love another baby as much as I loved Tanner. I wasn't ready to take on the responsibility of another child, but was starting to get used to life throwing a curve ball at me every time I would start to settle into a new normal. Acceptance was my only option, and again, I took a deep breath and continued trudging forward.

The day Connor was born, my fears of not being able to love another child instantly vanished as I held him in my arms. God had given me another reason to keep going, to keep moving forward. I was so deeply grateful for these two little boys who lit up my world every time I looked at them. Although I felt the comfort of God's hand within my children, postpartum depression had kicked in and taken control of my mind and body. I couldn't pull myself out of bed in the morning anymore. I would lie in bed all day and go for days without showering. The anti-depressants completely numbed all feeling and emotion, and I felt the end of my life drawing closer and closer. I often found myself thinking of ways to end my life, but my boys were always my reason to keep fighting. I felt completely trapped in this life, and couldn't see any way of ever getting out.

One day my doctor gave me a prescription that I believe saved my life. She told me to get outside of my house everyday, even if that meant just stepping out onto my front porch. I promised her I would do this, and I slowly began making baby steps outside of my house, taking the boys on small walks, and eventually I found myself one day standing in front of a gym. I took the boys into the free daycare provided by the gym and they ran off to play with all the toys. I looked around the gym and was drawn to a door in the corner. As I walked through the door, I found myself stepping into my first yoga class. I quietly grabbed a yoga mat and made my way to the back corner of the classroom. I didn't want to talk to anyone; I wanted to remain invisible. As the class proceeded, a deep calm rushed through my entire body, and a real smile crept across my face. I felt truly happy for the first time in a long time, perhaps ever. I felt like I had connected to a part of me that was bigger than any experience I had ever gone through. I felt whole and complete for just a moment.

Going to yoga became a daily routine for me. It became that same creative outlet I had felt as a ballerina so many years before. It gave me a chance to connect with a sense of happiness that was buried deep within. Before long, I stopped taking the anti-depressants and I was able to feel again. I made a promise to myself that I would never use an anti-depressant again. I would rather feel all the pain of my emotions than be numb to it.

It wasn't long after that Daryn, my little girl, entered my world; and once again, I was given the magic ability of loving someone more deeply than I could ever imagine. She instantly became everyone's sunshine. She stole and softened the heart of her father, and her brothers took on the responsibility of protecting her at all costs. She was such a little spitfire right from the very beginning; she entered this world with a personality of a true warrior. I knew no one would ever have the ability to dictate her life the way I felt my life had been, and I admired this quality within her.

For the first time, I felt I was starting a new chapter of my life. My family was complete and it was my turn to discover who I was. I asked Ken if I could participate in a yoga teacher training course, and he laughed it off, saying it was a waste of time and money. This was just the push I needed to make my dream a reality. Once again, my rebellious side kicked in and I was out to prove to Ken and the world that I could become a yoga instructor. And just like that, I was pregnant again. This time, the news hit me like a ton of bricks. Once again, my life and dreams would be put on hold, and I felt the vice of my world closing in around me again. As the depression slowly crept back in, I began to mourn the loss of my dreams once more. My marriage had turned into years of conflict and was completely unfulfilling. I knew I had checked out years ago, but I didn't know how to physically get out. I felt trapped, stuck, paralyzed. My yoga practice and study of yogic philosophy began to pull me further and further away from the religion in which I'd grown up. The Mormon teachings no longer resonated as truth to me; however, my entire life still revolved around it. My friends, neighbors, community, and family were all Mormons. This wasn't something I could just walk away from. I was in way too deep. I was struggling with so much internal conflict as Mason was born, yet I was given another incredible gift from God, a reason to keep fighting, to keep pushing the boundaries of what was. Mason was such a happy baby. He was born with an independence and ability to have no fear of anything. He showed me that life didn't have to be so serious all the time. He became my constant reminder to laugh and play through the struggles and hardship. Mason also taught me extreme patience, as he was always pushing the boundaries with me, reminding me who was actually in charge.

One Sunday morning I was teaching a Sunday School lesson to the children of our church. The lesson was about following the prophet, as he was the one who receives Divine revelation or guidance from God. I remember looking out into the audience and seeing the innocent faces of all the little children, but what struck me the hardest were my two boys, now six and seven years old, looking up at me with intent focus on what I was teaching. A voice inside told me that this wasn't what I wanted my boys to grow up believing. I knew internally that God dwelled within all of us, and that no man had control over our lives. We were the creators of our lives, and we only needed to go within to receive guidance and answers. I immediately walked off the stage and informed another teacher that I couldn't finish the lesson. I walked away from the only belief system I had ever known that day. It was one of the most liberating feelings I have ever felt, but this feeling was very short-lived. I was met with much judgement, criticism, and disapproval from my family, church community, and friends. I felt instantly alone in the world again. It was the same feeling I had felt as a child, not having anyone to lean on for strength. I was once again forced to turn within and lean on that part of myself that was stronger than any experience or circumstance in this life.

By this time, I knew I needed to find a way to support my four kids. I had a sinking feeling in my gut that my marriage was coming to an end, and I was stepping into a huge life transition. I quickly became certified as a yoga instructor and started teaching classes all around the community, and I also took my first Reiki certification course. I knew this wasn't enough to support my kids on my own and was constantly searching for what my next step would be. One day as I was driving down the street, I noticed a massage school. A force within me turned my car into the parking lot of the school, and I found myself walking in to check things out. Within less than 30 minutes, I was enrolled in massage school, handed a stack of text books, and walking back out to my car. I stood by my car, looking at the text books and thought to myself, 'what in the hell just happened? And how am I going to tell Ken what I've just done?'

I came home, put on my brave face, and courageously told Ken that I would be starting massage school the following Monday morning. He could support me or leave me, but either way I was doing this. Ken had no choice but to support me, and this was the beginning of finding my passion and love for healing the body. During this time, I was on a deep transformational journey of healing myself emotionally and spiritually, and I had many profound experiences with healers throughout my community, as well as completing another yoga teacher training certification. I loved learning about the human anatomy, and found so much joy in my schooling and studies. A whole new world had opened up before me. I graduated from massage school exactly one year after enrolling, and opened a little massage room in the back of a yoga studio downtown. That same week, I told Ken I wanted a divorce, and moved myself and the kids into my parents home. This was a very confusing time for both of us, and eventually Ken and I moved back in together to try and give our marriage one last try. Two more years of struggling to make things work, and this time we both knew the marriage was over. We separated and were divorced within two months.

I tried stepping into the painfully daunting task of dating, and quickly realized that I wasn't very good at it. I had been married for 15 years and didn't know the first thing about dating or choosing a partner. After dating a few men, I met Matt. He seemed to be a great catch, and I thought we had a lot in common; we both loved the outdoors and hiking. I was extremely lonely during this time and searching for anyone or anything that would fill that void. During our very short period of dating, I would often get an internal gut feeling that I needed to keep my distance and not get too close to him, but my loneliness overruled my internal guidance system and I found myself breaking every rule I had set for myself around dating someone. I was out hiking one morning trying to clear my head, and I felt an all too familiar feeling within. I rushed into town and bought a pregnancy test and my fears were confirmed. I was pregnant AGAIN! How on earth had I allowed this to happen again??? I must be some kind of complete idiot! I raged at myself internally as the reality began to sink in. "Good job Jen! You have completely managed to fuck up your entire life!" I hadn't spoken to Matt in over a month, and now I had to call him and deliver the news. I was so embarrassed, ashamed, and broken. I had definitely hit rock bottom and could see no way of pulling myself back up. Something was different about this pregnancy from all the others; the instant bond I had felt with my other pregnancies just wasn't there.

Sometimes the answers we seek aren't always the answers we think we'll find, but I received a clear knowing within that I wasn't to be this baby's mother, and I made one of the hardest decisions I have ever made in my life. Two days before Christmas, I drove alone to Salt Lake City, met my sister in tears, and used all the money I had saved up for my kids' Christmas to have an abortion. No one can ever explain the sense of loss, emptiness, and complete grief that a woman goes through during this process. I had never mourned this deeply in my entire life. The guilt, shame, and anger I processed through were truly some of the toughest emotions I have ever felt in my life. Again, I was alone in the world with no one to lean on but my big sister. She became my life raft, my anchor, my saving grace. I rallied around my four kids and began to show them a love and support deeper than I had ever shown them. They were my reason for living, and I felt that If I could love them deeply enough, this spirit that I carried for a short time would somehow feel that love as well.

I had given up on finding a man that would cherish and love me. After all, I didn't deserve to be loved. I had fucked up so many times in my life, how could anyone love me through all my baggage and flaws? I have learned that the Universe always has such a mischievous way of working her magic, and just as I had given up on myself, Lon showed up in my life.

As much as I tried to push him away and ignore that he was there, he persistently and patiently waited for me to slowly take down the walls I had built around my heart. I have never been loved so deeply by someone in my entire life. He saw a light deep within me that I thought had been burned out long ago. He saw me for who I truly was when I couldn't see it within myself. After dating for a year, we were married in the fall of 2012, and my life has truly been a fairytale since. Well, mostly…

One month after our marriage, I woke up one morning in extreme back pain. I tried everything from massage to acupuncture to chiropractic care, but nothing would ease the pain, and it continued to get worse as the days and weeks rolled by. I finally found myself facing back surgery and I worried that I may never do yoga, massage, or hike again. The day they wheeled me into surgery, I felt as though I had failed myself in some way. There must be some other way to cure my back pain. Every part of my being felt out of alignment with doing surgery, but I couldn't see any other option. I needed to get my back healthy again. The surgery went as expected, and I slowly gained back my strength and started practicing yoga and hiking again. Not long after my back had healed, I started to get extreme pain in my right knee. I hadn't injured myself, and couldn't think of anything that would be causing so much pain in my knee. Again, after trying all types of treatment to ease the pain, I sat down one day in complete frustration. I was finally living the life I had always dreamed of, and my body was starting to fall apart. I went into a meditation, and received the awareness that the pain coming from my knee and my back was emotional pain. I started to focus on the pain in my knee and began asking it questions. I discovered this pain to be guilt and shame. As I thought about all the times in my life I had experienced these emotions, I slowly started to feel the pain run down my leg, through my foot, and out my toes. I thought I must be going crazy, but I continued working through the emotions that were coming up until the pain was completely gone.

The pain in my knee has never come back. I knew I was onto something, and I started to play around with this technique with a few trusted friends. One day, a friend of mine called me from California. She was getting ready to go on a hiking trip, and had a bad pain in her knee. She said she didn't really know why she was calling me to help as I was in Utah, but I told her I wanted to try something. This was the first time I had tried this technique via long distance. The next day she called me to let me know her knee pain was completely gone. And this was the start of creating my own therapy called *Emotional Balancing*.

Each one of us is built with an internal guidance system and we have the ability to heal ourselves on a physical, emotional, and spiritual level once we learn how to tap into this part of ourselves. All the answers we seek come from within. We are all intuitive, and we all receive messages, inspiration, and Divine guidance from our Higher Selves. It is my belief that disease comes from negative emotions, thoughts, or belief patterns that we hold within. These negative emotions can become trapped within the body, keeping us in a state of dis-ease. We have the ability to release and let go of all negative thoughts or emotions. The body is completely designed to heal from all dis-ease. We heal ourselves through shifting our thought patterns, emotions, and vibrational state. Each emotion holds a gift or a message from the Higher Self. The moment we become aware of the emotion and allow ourselves to connect with it, we receive the message or gift, and the emotional pattern is broken.

I have learned that the highest kingdom of heaven, as well as the depths of hell, reside within us, and we must know them both in order to truly know ourselves. We have chosen to come into this life in order to experience both ends of the spectrum. We must know darkness in order to see the light. We must know pain and sorrow in order to know healing and happiness. We must know fear in order to know love.

Each one of the people who have played a leading roll in the drama of my life have become my greatest teachers. As I reflect back over my past, everything I've gone through has shaped me into the person I am today. I am grateful for my upbringing as a Mormon, for it has taught me to believe in a power much greater than myself; and though we may call it by different names, God, the Universe, Source Energy, Higher Self...this energy resides within each of us. When you connect to the God-energy that lies within, you have the ability to truly heal your life.

Emotional Balancing has become my greatest passion in life. I am grateful to be sharing my gifts and knowledge with others by providing *Emotional Balancing* sessions in person, as well as remotely to my clients all over the globe. I hope to someday travel the world and teach others how to connect with their Higher Self, release the trapped emotions that have kept them stuck, and help break the cycle of dis-ease, pain, and suffering. In the Bhagavad Gita, we are told that we transcend our suffering to the degree that we are able to passionately employ our gifts in the service of others. It is my greatest desire to bless as many people as possible with the gift of truly knowing themselves.

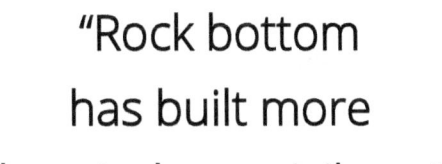

"Rock bottom
has built more
hero's than privilege."

~ Mel Robbins

CHAPTER THREE

Take Responsibility

By Ryan Roth

Maybe my experiences have taught me a few things which might impact you, by giving you some headaches.

But where to begin....

Absentee father, alcoholic grandfather, unsupportive mother, abusive brother...now all of those things could be things I could easily blame and use for excuses for not achieving anything in my life, but it's all about context; it's all about how our choices run, about how we take things which happen in our lives. Or, I guess it's best to say, it's all subjective.

Now I possess one quality which is apparently extremely rare, but, again, when I say what it is, you will think it's negative. Let me explain, but first I'll say I've achieved some measure of success, which you can judge for yourself, and I guess I'd not be in this book unless I had achieved something.

I'm likely to be the most repressed person you will ever meet in your life.

I studied psychology and law at university and, while in a psychology class, we were all given a test which measures certain personality traits. After a few days passed, many nights out and a great deal of alcohol (I was a student after all), I was asked to come into a meeting. So, I asked a few of my classmates when their meetings were and realised it was only me who had to meet with faculty, and what happened next was a little strange. My friends thought I was in trouble while I just thought it was a meeting, and I could see concern in them. I guess that was kind of a sign of what was to come.

So, there I was, walking to meet my maker with a sense of foreboding and a little sense of guilt: the kind you have when you know you've done nothing wrong, but a police car is behind you.

Sitting down, it was just one lecturer... then another... then another... then all of my lecturers. Okay, something was up. What the hell was going on? Why were they all here?

They then started to ask me a series of questions about my childhood, and so I told them about my alcoholic grandfather, but, by the way, he was amazing. He just liked to drink and was always happy. So, my experience with alcoholism has always been positive, and the Irish in me loves a great single malt, while the English in me loves a glass of gin (Ki No Bi as my preference), while the German in me doesn't like beer. And then there was my brother. Okay, you live with the school bully who's four years older, and you get a few slaps as a kid and go to A&E a few times, and you have all of his enemies turning their anger toward you when he graduates. Okay, it's not easy, but you deal with it. My mother was good in her own way, and she'd give me anything she had, but she didn't support or encourage me in any way. And I remember her saying two things: "Don't go to university;" and "One day you could be a store manager of a convenience store." Not exactly encouraging, right?

Then there was my father. Well, that's a mess of a situation and one hell of a colourful character, the kind of person that takes charge of the entire room, who brings life to it, who makes you happy from just being around him, but an absentee figure in my life who lied to me. And, so, when I was 15 years old, I told him, "I don't want you in my life. Don't call. Don't make excuses. You lied to me." It's not important what about, but I'm including this to build the image of what I came from.

My mother had nothing while my father had immense wealth, and I decided I would never have bad people around me, even if it was my father, and I never accepted any money from him.

So, why is none of that bad?

Why I do not care about any of the negative in that? Well, my brother is now a good friend and is my brother. He grew out of being a bully and has his own construction company, which I'm very proud of. My father would later go through various people to get in touch, to offer me to take over his multi-national, which I refused, and all of these family experiences taught me something.

- The only person accountable for your life is you. There are no excuses.

My lecturers explained to me that these hard conditions remove what most people have, and they're called coping mechanisms, such as money, home, food, friends, family, etc.

I/We had no money. I went hungry some nights and ate cooking apples, knowing I would be sick from eating them. I was isolated from friends as my brother was the school bully, so why would you want to be friends with his brother? I had no family stability except for my grandfather, and our home was a rental home and some months we had no money to pay the rent.

When you remove the normal coping mechanisms of a child, you create a different engine, a different kind of person when it comes to coping with extreme situations.

So, what I've been told, and it seems to have held up over the years, is, no matter the situation, big or small, I simply fix the problem/situation first and then think about it more after. I never get stressed, never freak out. No problem is too big, and I never get flustered on stage. While, to be honest, as a kid I'd look like a cooked lobster if I lost my lines reading in public. It was not a pretty sight, but even that was good, and I guess it links back to my past.

If something scares me or if I'm not very good at it, I do it until it doesn't scare me or I'm at least okay at it. It turns out in the end that I'm not so bad at the old public speaking lark, and I do seem to thrive in public debates. I was signed to the London Speakers Bureau in March of 2018, and they represent some huge names, so I was very humbled to accept. When I was 33, I even gave the keynote at the National Stadium in Beijing on the future of urban design. I was not supposed to give the keynote, but being around some people with huge reputations in architecture, they asked me to make the address, and wow! what an experience from a kid who was never even trained as an architect, who had 400 architects working for him, and as a child who would avoid any kind of public speaking.

What I also noticed over the years is that I seem to deconstruct everything—and I mean everything. But what do I mean? Okay, so where does your water come from? How is it paid? What kind of material are the pipes built from? Why is your wooden table so cheap? Why did that politician say what he said? What financial support does he get? What are his real intentions? Who owns the news company I'm reading? Why is that farmer so poor? Why does a cup of coffee cost $3 when you get 120 cups of espresso from 1kg of coffee, and yet the farmer gets $0.01 to $0.03 per cup? Why is there a COP 23? How have they not solved these issues yet? How was the WWF formed? (Okay, this one is crazy.) How has Greenpeace failed?

I believe having a highly active desire for information from any and all areas, my ability to break things down, and being repressed in this sense I've stated above, has allowed me to achieve what I have. But what have I achieved?

So, now you know a little of my past, but why have I been asked to write this chapter?

Well, you can gauge this for yourself.

I had my first companies at age 11 (distribution and logistics), then at 15 (betting with my grandfather on horses and tennis), and then at 19. No need to go into details about these companies at 11 and 19, but I will say that they made a fair bit of money and in many senses were original. The one at 19 was using a Spanish project to print calendars super cheap but high quality. The Spanish government subsidised this production plant, as it would hire I think recovering meth and heroin addicts to prove they can be functional members of society. This meant we could produce a calendar cheaper than anyone else in the UK, and no one knew how we could do it. This was only possible as a friend of mine is Spanish and knew of the project, and, so, I saw an opportunity.

Now these were all small endeavors, but they gave me a sense of belief, a sense of opportunity to achieve bigger things.

Skip a few years later and we're now going past Uni, into the Unknown. I know what the world looks like according to the BBC, but what does it actually look like? Let's travel a little. Ummm, maybe a lot.

As a kid growing up with my mother, I was racist, which I think all people generally are, as you have stereotypes or beliefs about other races, which can be of different races or your own, and it's only bad when what you're doing is negative. Now, as a kid, I noticed that my mother really didn't like foreigners taking British jobs, as that's what it would say in the tabloids, and this started to affect me, but I had no foreign friends and so my views were from my mother. This changed when I was dating a lovely girl from the Philippines while I was in college, and my mother was—let's say—not a fan. So, I told her if she didn't stop being racist I'd not speak to her for three years. Three years later, she was not racist anymore, and the moment I met people of different races, I wasn't racist myself.

•Our parents' views will affect us, but we must have our own opinions.

So, now we move on to the next chapter of my life. My foray into humanitarian work, which I won't go into with many details, but I'll give the highlights.

Arrogant kid looks to change the world on his own without knowing how the world works. I lost.

I was doing the most mentally taxing humanitarian work that exists. Going into detail about this would kill your vibe. The majority of the population do not want to discuss this subject/issue, as it's so bad. While I was doing this for three years, I met a wonderful girl who gave me a great deal of support mentally, as it would take me three months or so to get back to myself after the world I was in. I was living in Paris at the time and working in Asia. It was a beautiful, sad period of my life, during which I grew a great deal because of the relationship I was in. I was no longer the arrogant kid by the end of this relationship, and I grew. I'll explain later why I've mentioned this past relationship. She was a great girl for whom I wish the very best and if I never told her then, I say now, thank you for all you gave me.

Now the business side starts to get going and fun times are ahead.

I moved to Sydney and looked to build a hotel in Papua, New Guinea, where I think I still have the land rights for a few more years. This project was simply too much for me at that age as I'd never factored in weather patterns. I had a great time and learned a lot. At a dinner one night in PNG, my friend said while laughing his arse off, "Just so you know," motioning to this other guy who was sitting next to me, "he ate someone two weeks ago. His village cooked and ate another tribesman." So, in PNG it was an adventure, horror story, scattered with extreme beauty and savagery. But after a few years in Sydney, I wanted a change. So, the day before my birthday, I decided to move to LA.

What would America have to offer? This is the place where all the kids feel they know more than their own country. After all, this is what we saw in the movies.

The first night in America was interesting. I remember getting off the plane, feeling so hot—August 15th—not really dressed for the weather and feeling entirely alone. Having a late flight in, meant an airport hotel would be the best bet.

Writing about this is bringing back so many memories, so many experiences, and I'm remembering strange, random situations like the time my friend, Darren Darnborough, got drunk with Mark Ruffalo (The Hulk), and my first words to him were, "You sucked in X movie. What were you thinking?" He laughed. He knew the movie was terrible and said, "Oh it was my friend's movie." Or, that's what my mind remembers him saying. We all had a great laugh and way too many drinks that night. I remember all three of us, or maybe it was just Darren, taking jumping photos.

I could go on and on about the escapades I had in LA but will simply say it was something that shaped me, and it's a place dear to my heart, but it's not where my heart is.

I found LA to be an intense mess of chaos, desperation, debauchery, endless hope, dreams, vanity, acceptance, betrayal, rumours, shallow, warm, loving, and not part of the real world. After all, they call it LA LA LAND.

I decided I wanted to see if I could act, and I got 90% of the roles I went for, but at the time, I was not on the right visa, so it was more a test to myself or maybe my hubris.

While in LA, I decided to start a DJ and band management company, which went very well, but it took so much time, and my life was a long, long party. I felt bored but was making great money and was even offered a job for $35,000 a month, which I turned down, as it would be more of the same.

Then I was asked by one of my closest friends, Ron Truppa, to be part of the first directorship of the Catalina Film Festival, and so I just said yes. I remember he was surprised I'd just say yes so quickly. This was a guy who let me crash on his couch for, I think, two weeks or four weeks—I forget—but a great guy who's always been there for me, with an amazing wife and his family. Just wow! His family made me think of what I thought a family should be like. An Italian-American family, full of life and endless amounts of food to consume. Ron Truppa, Sr., my friend's father, makes great wine at home, while Lori, his mum, has a dodgy hip I make fun of, in jest, of course. These are people who I drink too much wine with when we hang out, and just this Christmas we all video called with silly graphics.

Now, since I've mentioned Ron, I should also mention Anna. These are two of my closest friends in LA, two people I can always rely on, who I speak to regularly, and I've not been in LA for seven or eight years now, and still they're extremely dear to me. Distance and friendship have no bearing on one another.

•Value good friends. Remove any negative friendships from your life.

So, I helped Ron and Delious start the Catalina Film Festival, which is a top five film festival in the US and one of the top 40 managed events in all of the US.

But being in LA, being bored with this nightlife existence, I decided I wanted to stop working in music and transfer what I'd learned to artists, painters in particular, and I decided I should move to Tokyo or Bali. And this is where I think my life opened a whole new chapter, or I guess it was the start of a whole new book, and where I met the most important person of my life.

One day, something shifted in me and it was, I believe, the day after the New Year. Now I've had these things happen before and the best way I can explain it would be to say that every seven or so years I seem to have a deeper understanding of life. It happens more frequently now, but something shifted in me and, right at that moment, I met the most wonderful woman of my life, who would change it forever. This is where Yuki entered my life.

When we met, I was living in LA and she was in Tokyo, but as I was about to move to Bali or Tokyo, this wasn't a factor. To make a long story short, I moved to Tokyo and set up an art management company with an art gallery on the 47th floor of a building from which you could look over Tokyo Harbour, Tsukiji Fish Market, and even the Emperor's Palace.

While walking along the streets one night with Yuki, I saw a very small sticker, and at first glance it looked like trash on the wall, but, looking more closely, I saw that it was one of the most subtle and amazing artworks I'd ever seen, and still is to this day. It was a piece called *I Hate Rain* by 281 Anti Nuke, and in that moment we decided to contact him. We signed him to the agency right away. Now, I couldn't have signed him without Yuki, as the language barrier was such an issue for me, but she added a gentler and kinder side, which I guess back then I lacked.

A few days later, we had Channel 24 from France flying in to interview 281, then newspaper after newspaper. Vice came to film a documentary on him, where I had a solid 20 seconds of fame, but it was these moments and instances which really started to define the company.

Shortly after, I decided that instead of showing his works in a gallery, I'd show his works in the Foreign Correspondents' Club in Tokyo. As his work was political, it made so much sense for me to exhibit there to gain the most exposure. The exhibition was the most successful they had ever had, even resulting in his work being on the front page of a Syrian newspaper when the Syrian conflict broke out.

I was up against it, only charging artists 20%, rather than the 50% other galleries were charging, so you can imagine the number of requests we'd get for representation. It was just crazy. One, two, five, ten artists a day were seeking representation. For a while there, I'd look at the artists, have meetings, dinners, etc. But maybe it was my own hubris creeping back in with the success we were having, which blinded me to how much time I was wasting and how much of my time was spent working and not living. This would come back to bite me later, but during that whole time I had the most amazing support any man could ask for.

I remember this one moment when I decided to open the gallery and Yuki said, "It might take some time to make money, but I will take a full-time job to make sure we're okay and you can focus on building the company." We'd not known one another very long, but I'd never felt this kind of love and support in my life.

Luckily, we made profit from day two with art sales, a little luck, and a lot of hard work, and I would not have been able to build it without her.

Back then it was such an interesting and strange time. We were living in what I'd best describe as a shoebox, but it was our shoebox. Living in a place I still think about as home, a place we felt so happy to just do simple things like running along the river in Sakura season, playing with our kind of adopted cat, Sticky, going for long walks at night, eating Japanese curry with Naan bread the size of a small child, or just staying at home and eating something wonderful she whipped up.

I was starting to know what had been missing in my life, starting to understand that family is something I'd never had, but she was that for me, and I could say for the first time I was in love.

- Have balance in your life and live today. Plan for the future, but don't sacrifice the present.

Now 281 was something defining in my life for a number of reasons, but his identity was what was important and, to this day, I'm the only person in the world to know his real identity, unless he's told anyone himself and—please bear in mind—in Japan, street art is illegal, and if he was ever caught, his whole life would be destroyed.

Cutting his story short, he was targeted by right-wing groups in both Japan and the US.

They started hunting him down on his social media accounts, hacking his and our email and our websites. Our websites were rarely up as a result.

Death threats—and not any ordinary death threats, but some of the most graphic and violent things you could imagine. Phones calls would be 10% business and 90% threats, and at one point we had over 200 death threats in one day.

Thankfully, Yuki never got the business emails or phone calls, so I could keep that to myself, but it got to a point where organised groups were about to start hunting 281 where he usually placed his artworks, and so I needed to do something.

We did a subtle change to our website, which stated 281's real name. With all the online hunting going on, I wanted to place it on the site as if it was by mistake, and the moment we saw it on the hate group chat forums, we'd take it down and that's exactly what we did.

They took the bait, and after some weeks we put the name back on the site, as the cat was out of the bag. He now has the most generic name in Japan.

The police had almost arrested him, and a group got pretty close to finding out who he was, so we needed something else. And, so, like every Englishman, I decided it was time for some tea.

Every death threat would result in the following generic reply, "Today I'll be at X cafe at 1pm if you'd like to meet for tea and scones, and you can meet me face-to-face."

Each day I'd turn up, and each day I'd have my tea and scones alone.

Now, bear in mind what I spoke about before, about repression. I find if someone is going to do something, they won't announce it first; they will just do it.

Shortly after this, I wanted to build this into the story of 281, and so once a month I'd arrange a dinner for press, on my tab and inside the art gallery, which happens to be inside a one Michelin star restaurant. Thanks to my dear friend, Angelo, I had an art gallery inside one of the most expensive places in the whole world, with breathtaking views and food you could not imagine.

The gallery/restaurant was also my office and if I was there in the morning or before lunch, Angelo would go in the kitchen and make me something. We had this great little arrangement where he'd get rotating art once every three months, and I'd have a gallery, which no one else could ever afford to do. Come on, on the 47th floor overlooking Tokyo Bay, and it's my art gallery and not for some guy who's had a gallery before, just a kid who wanted to have a gallery which would look and feel like something you'd want/love.

- If you don't ask, you will never get anything.

Angelo is one of the most warm and friendly people you'd ever meet, and the success of the gallery was heavily impacted by him, a charming Italian guy who gave a new art dealer/gallery owner a chance.

So, one day I decided to start these monthly press dinners with a plan. The plan would be to quietly suggest stories to the press, surrounded by art, beautiful views over Tokyo, and an endless drinks bar. Angelo and his staff would come out with one delicious course after another, with wine, limoncello, and a host of other sumptuous drinks. While the staff was plying them with libations, I'd be quietly talking about the art world in general, but sprinkling rumours and stories about other artists, and one of them happened to be 281 Anti Nuke. "Did you know they call him the Japanese Banksy?"

A few weeks later, a friend called me from New York and said, "Ryan, have you read it?" to which I asked, "Read what?" *The New Yorker* declared 281 Anti Nuke "The Japanese Banksy."

While I had a great time entertaining the press those evenings in Tokyo looking over Tokyo at night, it was paying off, but it was also taking its toll on me. But more of that later.

In 2013, I'd be called one of the top 500 cultural influencers in the world to watch by *The Observer/Guardian,* and all that from a guy who had never studied art.

- If you have an idea of what you want, plan how you get there.

The gallery was doing well, and over the years we've been featured in hundreds of major news media outlets, but I was getting a little bored, and Yuki and I decided to move to Bangkok to start a new chapter.

While I was still there running the art gallery, I became very concerned about money. To make sure we were both okay, I was sacrificing the time I should have been putting into our relationship. I'd constantly break dinner dates, having business as an excuse, and without knowing it I was hurting the most wonderful woman I had ever known.

•Give time to your relationship and never break a promise. NEVER.

While in Bangkok, I was headhunted for an architecture firm, but I was not an architect. I had no training or real interest in this area, but I realised while being with Yuki those years that I was able to quickly adapt to any industry and I seem to have an ability to deconstruct and understand industries and problems while also being able to quickly have a solution.

After taking over an architecture firm of 400 architects, I quickly realised I couldn't get anything done. In the first week, it would take me one hour just to get to work, as everyone wanted to have a one-minute "Good morning, Mr. Roth. How was your evening?" Well, first I banned the name Mr. Roth so that everyone could just call me Ryan, but that didn't work. So, then I implemented three policies:

(1) Apart from saying good morning, don't look to have a chat with me in office hours;

(2) If you have a work-related matter, speak to one of three people who come to me or email me bullet points three times per week;

(3) I would only be in the office a few hours per week.

Now, these measures might seem extreme, but bear in mind, being the CEO of an architecture firm is a glorified sales role. I was the show pony, and if the show pony didn't perform, that's anything from 700 to 2000 people who will be going hungry, won't be able to pay their rent, and will have their cars repossessed.

- Don't take things personally.

No one was ever told why I implemented these conditions, only that I was busy. It also wasn't a huge shock as I was constantly flying all around Asia for client meetings. One of our clients even called an emergency meeting, as he said, "I must see you," and so I was on a plane the next day. This guy represented 30% of our client base and he knew it.

I flew in only for him to say, "It's very important. We must make dumplings." I'd flown from Bangkok to a remote area of China for this, and it was to make bloody dumplings with the execs of a fortune 500 company.

I was furious, and so I said, "Thanks for the dumplings, and if you pull this shit again, I'll add 20% onto your next invoice, and it will say, Ryan cooking dumplings." We all had a good laugh and he realised without me saying too much that I was willing to lose him as a client if he kept pushing his limits.

•Never let someone cross the line.

•Be willing to lose a client.

The architecture firm was a little bit early, as after increasing the size of the company and being asked to speak on some amazing panels, like the Shell Futures Cities program in Bangkok, I started to not only get more into the concept of human society and living by public debate.

On this panel, I'd have a debate with Shell's leading political advisor, which would result in him calling me an anarchist because of my views of what will happen in the future, but he could not disagree with me. I had a great time on that panel, which would later lead me to speak in China and be offered two professorships in both Beijing and Shanghai, which I turned down.

I was also a humble advisor to the Seasteading Institute and given a chance to speak at a separate event in Beijing on the future of architecture.

I was only due to speak at this event, but after spending time with the other architects, all with much bigger firms than mine, all having studied architecture and all older than me by at least 15 years, from places like Australia, Denmark, Holland, UK, China, Taiwan, and more, they all voted for me to give the keynote. What?

I never studied art, I never studied architecture, and I'm asked to give the keynote on the future of architecture. I felt like it was all some strange surreal dream and, to top it all off, I was to give the address at the Bird's Nest Stadium, one of the most iconic buildings in the world.

While I walked onto the stage, I had to quickly amend my talk and presentation which featured an Allan Watts speech about consumerism and featured footage, in a negative way, about the Chinese Army. So, I'm now in China, addressing government officials, giving a keynote speech about the future of architecture, and I end up giving a scathing speech about all my peers and criticising them all for using the phrase "green design," as there was no definition of this at the time. To top things off, in the audience was the Chinese undersecretary of the communist party, and here I am slamming all the architects in the audience and, true to form since I was a kid, I seem to speak up. And, so, I then went into the impact of false economies, ghost cities, and how the Chinese economy would have a semi-meltdown within six months.

Three months later, the Chinese economy took a massive hit. I was surprised I wasn't detained or something, to be honest, as growing up in the west, we're told so much about Chinese Communist oppression. But after I gave a few more speeches in China, I was offered two professorships and became known as the future of urban design, as I came up with a plan for urban living which would very cheaply convert a city into a place everyone would love to live, with private rooftop gardens for birds, trees on most streets to both create shade for the people and reduce heat capture on the concrete, and a number of other things.

- Be opinionated.

Writing about the Chinese speech reminds me of the public debate I had in 2017 where I was attacked by the heads of the US Consulate, Embassy, Golden Agri, and Monsanto (Indonesia). Four vs one. David won on that occasion, and it was more like a teacher talking to four schools' kids. I even called Monsanto out on being culpable for the suicide of 500,000 Indian farmers over 10 years. The audience looked at me in complete shock, as no one calls them out on their shit.

- Know what you're talking about.

I guess that's enough about my past, but what am I up to now?

Well, I'm the founder of TEDxCanggu, which will launch October 16, 2018, in Bali.

I asked two friends to be part of my core team. A full production company will provide sponsored coverage, and my head of communications just recruited her entire old PR company to come onboard. I feel I must be doing something right if all these people, much more talented than I am, have decided to jump onboard for no salary and just for the love of putting on a great event.

- Give the other person a fine reputation to live up to.
- When building a team, use the Mastermind Group concept.

A distillery might be made in the future, but that's a little way off and should be so much fun. I know nothing about the alcohol industry, but why would that stop me?

There is now a documentary series about to be filmed about me, and I can't wait. After some time accepting that it would be about me and being very dismissive about it, I've now begun to really enjoy the idea which would be part adventure, part conservation, and all about agriculture and food supply. More of that later.

I was recently signed to an organization I've wanted to represent me for many years, and so I emailed them about representing me for public speaking, and I was—and still am—humbled to be signed to the London Speakers Bureau, which represents some of the biggest names in the world from all industries, like Richard Branson, Buzz Aldrin, Usain Bolt, etc.

But now for the big one, a project so big it will change the face of the world.

With all my companies and some I've just not got enough time to discuss, like my branding company and others, I believe I can now see the world with something of an original gaze.

I saw something I wanted to change, and I saw just how to do it.

We're told global problems are too big for us to solve or the solution would be very complicated.

Well, that's just not true.

I've found how to solve global poverty and we're launching this new company in 2018. The people on my advisory team include Toni Patterson of Oatly and others. They'd not be behind me if they didn't think what I was doing was possible.

But I want you to really think about this, as I can't tell you what it's all about, only that the site is www.ka-bu.com @kabu_co and you should stay tuned.

I'm going up against the largest industry in the world, which is also the most important: the food industry.

If I'm right, we will also end the number one cause of climate change and poaching, and this company occupies most of my time these days.

Now, I could go on and list various other business experiences, but I will leave you with this.

I regret only one thing in my life, and that's that work was so all-encompassing that it started to make me unbalanced, and I was with the love of my life, a woman so good, so sweet, and so genuinely kind that she would cry all day if she broke a cup, "Ryan, it has a soul. It's been with us for so many years and shared so many moments with us."

I wasn't in perfect balance in my life, and I didn't live in the moments she tried for us to have, but instead I slowly destroyed our relationship.

The women I've mentioned in this chapter have moulded me, and I still have pieces of them in my personality, but Yuki made me who I am today.

I'd give up everything to go back and change those things I failed her on, to never break any of the little promises I made her, and to still have her beside me. She's still the only person in the world who could change my mind about anything, the person I would listen to more than anyone else, and the person I still to this day can say, "She is the best person I have ever known."

•Business success means nothing if you sacrifice those who matter the most to you.

Read random books about subjects which are not your usual interests, as you will start to think of your passionate subjects in a different way, and read books from different countries.

Have a little happiness every day. This is called *Ikigai* and something Yuki tried to teach me. *Ikigai* the book is available to buy.

•If nothing else in life, be kind.

"I know what it feels
like to completely hit
rock bottom and
have no clue how
you're going to pick
yourself back up.
It won't last forever."

~ Unknown

CHAPTER FOUR

Maintaining Resilience: Life after Rock Bottom

By Nicole Doherty

We pulled into the service station, and as my husband got out to fill the car, the smell of petrol filled my nostrils. I did my usual trick of locking all the doors. As I pressed the lock button, I noticed a young girl, about 15, sitting with her dog, eating an ice cream. I noticed everything about her, long brown curly hair, a blue dress and red cardigan. I couldn't see her face, but I didn't need to. From where I was sitting, she looked exactly like someone I used to know. Someone who had no fear. Someone who wore her bravado well, with a stiff upper lip. As I sat there, I started to cry. The girl reminded me exactly of me. Before... well, everything really. Before I completely lost my innocence.

My husband knocked on the window and I let him back in the car, I looked up at him and he noticed I was crying. By this stage I was bawling pretty hard, a good snotty nose, gut-wrenching cry. He asked what was wrong, and I couldn't answer. As we started to drive off, I pointed to the girl, but still couldn't speak. As we turned back onto the highway toward home, my mind racing, flashbacks hitting me like a tonne of bricks, my husband grabbed my hand, and again tried to find out what was wrong. I cried harder, one of those wounded cries. Words weren't coming, and I just shook my head.

As we pulled into our street, I knew I wasn't going to be able to walk. We turned into the driveway, my husband turned the car off, and turned to me again, pleading for me to tell him what was going on. It was about 10:30pm on a Wednesday night, and for some reason, the smell of petrol combined with seeing a young girl, who looked slightly like I did at a similar age, out at night seemingly with no fear, had completely triggered me - had thrown me into a tailspin of flashbacks, and I knew I was going to be sick. I looked at my husband, who was almost shaking me with concern, and I uttered the words I had never told another soul... "I think I was raped".

I should probably introduce myself: my name is Nicole Doherty, I'm a business owner, a mother, and a counsellor, and I can honestly say, it took a long time to be able to write these words. I had no idea, that this particular night, would be one of the biggest turning points in my life.

I can almost hear you thinking, 'how can someone "think" they were raped?' 15 years of solid drinking had certainly helped keep my mind as blank as possible. It certainly wasn't my only sexual assault, but it had been the trigger in a long battle with self medicating and risky behaviour. On this night though, all I had were pieces of flashbacks. After sitting in the car and talking until I had nothing else left to say, I managed to get inside the house, and collapse into bed. What followed were several days of nightmares, flashbacks, deep depression, and awkward conversations trying to fill in the blanks. Those blanks were not about the rape, but about something that happened five years previous, two days before my 11th birthday, when a homeless man attempted to kidnap and molest me at a train station.

You know when you know something is fact, but you can't really remember it? You think you can, but when you try and replay something in your mind, you realise the memories aren't yours. They are stories of other people who were there. Like being passed out drunk and hearing stories of the things you did the next day... you feel like you know that they happened, but when you try to think back, your memory is blank. That's what my kidnapping was like to me.

I knew the story off by heart, but I never realised that I didn't actually remember it. But after the petrol station incident, the flashbacks I experienced were vivid and terrifying. A few days later, I spoke to my Mum, and I told her about what I was remembering, about the assault and about the kidnapping. I had not seen my Mum cry that hard in a long time. I organised to see the statements from my kidnapping, so I could try and piece together what had happened.

My whole life, I had gone through traumas and just saddled myself up with baggage and just got on with it. I'd self-harmed, I'd tried to drink myself to death, but I still trudged through life with my armour of steel. Once the flashback's started, and by this point I was sober, I didn't have an addiction to turn to. I had no choice but to finally dig in, take time, and prepare myself for finally feeling the emotions that I had buried my whole life.

It was two days before my 11th birthday, and my little sister and I had been staying at my grandparents. My Nan arranged to travel on the train with us to where my Mum was picking us up, and we were all excited that Nan was coming down to stay for a week for my birthday. We arrived at the station, and I could see my Mum in the carpark. Running ahead, I hugged Mum, who told me to go put my bags in the boot while she went to help my Nan and little sister.

I reached the boot which Mum had left open and had just put my bags in when I could feel a presence. I had always been in tune with my own gut feelings, and I could feel that something was wrong. I sensed someone to my right, and as I looked up, I could see a dirty middle-aged man, coming through the rows of cars. I felt like my feet were made of concrete. Something didn't feel right. I looked up again, and saw he was much closer, and was pulling the zip of his filthy jeans down.

I felt the hairs stick up on the back of my neck. I felt sick. I was frozen. I screamed, but I don't remember hearing anything come out of my mouth. I closed my eyes in fear, hoping he would just walk past me, hoping I was just being silly... but then I felt it, his hands on my young body, down my top, something hard pressing into me. The smell of beer and urine filled my every cell.

Instinct kicked in, and I grabbed onto the back of the car. I stood my ground, dug in my heals, and I held on for dear life. But he was just too strong. He grabbed my hair, and dragged me across the carpark. I don't remember screaming, but somehow my Mum knew something was wrong and looked up to see me being dragged across the car park towards a group of men standing beside the river. In slow motion, I saw her running towards me. I had been taken less than 20 feet from her.

We had almost reached the other men, when somehow, I broke free. With my Mum running towards me, I finally found my feet, and started running towards her. But then I felt the hand grab me again, and smelt the stench of beer breath, as I was dragged backwards once again. His grubby hands were again grabbing me, touching me.

My next memory is of my Mum hitting him with all of her strength. Almost comically swinging her handbag towards his head, thumping against his skull. As he put his hands up to defend himself, he lost his grip on me again, and I ran around the other side of my Mum hoping she would protect me. My Nan arrived beside her, and starting laying in to him as well, a 4-foot-nothing little old lady, swearing at him like a sailor.

I heard laughing, and remember looking over at the men beside the river, who were all laughing heartily at the scene before them. None of them made any attempt to move. They all looked filthy, toothless, bearded, and drunk. The man retreated towards them, backing away from my Mum and Nan, who by this stage were hysterical with rage and fear. But he didn't leave. None of them left. They stood there menacingly, staring at me and my little eight year-old sister. I still felt sick... and instinctively stood in front of my sister to shield her from view.

From there, I remember people. I remember people standing around watching. A man in the car next to us. Not helping. I remember my Mum yelling at him. Then I remember being bundled into the back of a supermarket, while we waited for the police. As my attacker and his friends stood staring at us from across the carpark, I remember being given a can of coke... and thinking back, it makes sense why I reach for coke for comfort, even now.

The distant memories of the police, the station, giving statements, sitting in the children's sexual crime room waiting to talk, are all mostly a blur. But even 25 years later, when I attend the same station and sat in the same room to support clients who've reported their own sexual assaults, I remember it, trying not to have a panic attack.

The rest of the day remains a blur to me, until my Dad comes home with a broken hand, and I learn that the police have told him they would let my attacker back out at the train station in four hours when he sobers up. Those were the days where police sometimes encouraged vigilante justice when they couldn't do much within the confines of the law. I am forever grateful that my Dad was able to stop when he did, or this story could be very different.

It is little wonder that the people I look up to the most, who I see as my hero's, not just on this day, but throughout my whole life, are my parents and my Nan. It is also why I was never able to tell my Dad later of my rape... even to this day. I was scared that the next time he wouldn't stop, and it would be him that ended up in prison...because the law didn't always work.

Looking back now, after reading police statements, speaking to my Mum, and with the flashbacks allowing me to re-create exactly what happened in my mind, it is little wonder my brain decided it was best to blank most of this out in order to keep me safe... and also little wonder why my own career in the legal sector lasted less than six months.

As I write all of this out now, I'm filled with some sort of mixed emotions between pride and disbelief. These first 1500 words or so are enough to make me realise that I have been through a lifetime of trauma in my 37 years on this earth. When I first started jotting down ideas about what I wanted to share, so many things came to mind. As I was searching for a central theme of what my chapter would be about, the word 'resilience' immediately came to my mind. If I had to pick a word to describe myself, it would certainly be resilient. This book is about re-building your life from Rock Bottom; and as I write, I realise I am not even close to getting to my Rock Bottom, or to my eventual triumphs. But resilience after each and every set back is exactly who I am at my core. Over time, I have learnt to let in vulnerability and rawness, and the lessons continue hard and fast.

When I think about life's lessons, I am reminded how comical life can be. I am reminded that where there is light, there must also be darkness. Where there is love, there is also hate. Where there is a sunrise, there is also an inevitable sunset. Where there is life, there is also death. Where there is self-care, there is also self-harm.

The two biggest things that kept me alive at the age of 16 were meditation and self-medication; my self-care and my self-harm.

After my rape, life became unbearable. I became hardened. My complete innocence was gone, and in its place were distrust, anger, bitterness, and self-hatred. How could I have put myself in that position? We talk a lot about victim-blaming these days, but what any victim will tell you is that nobody could possibly blame themselves more than we do. Why didn't I see it coming? Did I lead them on? Did I do something to deserve this? As you attempt to scrub yourself from the inside out, the blame game begins.

Then, the self-harm begins. I remember scrubbing my pelvic region so hard with a scrubbing brush that I actually ripped skin... and it felt good. I was already bleeding, so why not rip the skin and really make a mess of it. Maybe then nobody will want to come near me. I could only hope.

My Mum used to drink Wild Peach Cask Wine on special occasions, family barbeques, birthdays, etc, and I had been allowed to have some a few months earlier on my 15th birthday. My friend Danielle had stayed over, our birthdays were two days apart, and we were allowed to have a little Vegemite jar sized glass of the wine as our first adult drink. We later snuck another, and I had developed a bit of a taste for the sweet peach nectar. I started drinking almost daily. I often filled my water bottle with half wine and half water and took it to school, just to 'take the edge off'.

Around this time, I made a new best friend, Corinne, who was a year older. I started going to parties with her and her friends, and drinking was certainly our favourite past time. As time passed, we started hitting pubs and nightclubs. I was underage, but my drunken confidence almost always got me in everywhere I wanted to go.

One night, we had been drinking with friends and decided to head out. We had drunk a whole 4-litre cask of Moselle between the two of us. Heading into town, I started feeling sick, and vomited all over myself and the back of the taxi. Corinne had the bright idea that we would tell the driver to pull over, so we could walk the rest of the way because we wanted some air. Luckily my pure bile stomach acid vomit had not started to smell yet, and the taxi driver did not suspect a thing.

A few hours later I woke up. I had no idea where I was. I tried to sit up, but my head was killing me. I realised that I was topless and missing a shoe. I was freezing cold, and alone. Then I heard someone groan, and vomit. As my eyes adjusted to the dark, I realised it was Corinne. I managed to stand up, and tried to look around in the dark for my top, cardigan and my other shoe. Then I remembered we had washed my clothes and hung them over a tree. I walked around the building, and as I got to the front, I realised we were at a church. I felt mortified. So disrespectful!

Walking around, I found the tree with my clothes and got dressed. I woke Corinne and tried to piece together what had happened. It was then that she realised she had been using my shoe as a pillow. We worked out that we had both been really sick, and the taxi had dropped us off outside the church. We decided that the only thing stopping us from still going nightclubbing was the vomit on my clothes. We looked around for a tap, washed my singlet and cardigan, hung them over a tree to dry, and then took a nap... or passed out.

Once we had made ourselves decent again, we decided it would be respectful to say a prayer. Neither of us were religious, but we made something up, picked up our things, and began to walk into town to the local nightclub. Luckily, a friend spotted us, told us everything was shut and drove us home... not my proudest moment.

Drinking had become my escape... every Thursday, Friday and Saturday night, I went to parties or clubs. During the week, I drank in small doses to take some of the pain I was feeling away... and to take away some of the shaking I was experiencing.

At the same time, my mum had started to notice something was not right, and decided to take me to a meditation class. Her friends had opened a wellness studio, and they were holding weekly sessions. I quickly learnt that meditation was my new escape. I used it daily. This was the mid 1990's, nobody my age was meditating! So I would meditate at school by hiding in the toilets. If anything saved my life, it was meditation. I learned to go deep quickly, and I learned to do it anywhere. I also learned the art of manifesting, of putting things out into the universe. I attended classes weekly, and quickly realised the benefits of switching off my mind. I completed *A Course In Miracles*, and I learned of famous personal development pioneers such as Tony Robbins.

Meditation is still a practice that I love. I use it in a very different way than I did in those early days, but I am forever grateful to my Mum's meditation group. I fear that without it, my drinking would not have been enough, and I would've found more extreme ways to cope.

It wasn't until I met someone that would turn out to be more self-destructive than I was, that I realised how lucky I truly was to have meditation in my life so I could share it. Christian Doherty.

I had moved out of home, from my small town near Geelong, to the big smoke of Melbourne, Australia. I had started going out to see bands, and a friend had asked me to go along to see her boyfriend's band. My friends and I arrived to the dodgiest pub in Collingwood, and when the band started to play, I was in love... death metal... the most extreme music I had ever heard. I was mesmerised by the lead guitarist, and chatted with him afterwards. Something told me that he was as troubled as I was. I later found out I was very right. We became firm friends, and bonded over our shared issues and eventually fell in love, which was the last thing either of us expected at the time. Both of us were alcoholics. Christian was a self-destructive drunk, and I was a self-medicating drunk. What a pair. One thing we knew for sure though, was that the stars had aligned, and we were meant to be. I had never trusted anyone the way I trusted Christian, and we opened up about our pasts, our traumas, and most importantly, we helped each other heal.

Ten years later, we've been through a lifetime of stuff together: nine years of marriage, several miscarriages, highs, lows, prosperity, close to bankruptcy, close to homelessness, close to suicide, depression, anxiety, sobriety and so much more. We are each other's rock, and each other's twin soul. There is nobody else on earth like this man, to me.

Just before our wedding, I decided to buy the company that I had been working for. I had been working in Community Services since 2001, mostly in the disability sector. The company was going under, and I couldn't bare to see the staff put off, or the clients, who mostly relied on us to get them out of bed, just left without care.

I'd had discussions with a few other staff who were interested in buying in, when the bookkeeper put in a bid at the last minute, and took me along for the ride. Little did I know at the time, this business would be my greatest success, and my greatest undoing, both mentally and financially.

A few years passed, and we slowly started to build the business. However, while I was very client and staff-focused, she was very financially-focused, and we clashed constantly. I was told there was not enough money to sustain the both of us, and after being bullied relentlessly, I just physically could not continue. With the years of trauma and alcohol abuse, coupled with flailing mental health, once the flashbacks and nightmares had begun, I just couldn't cope any longer. I had split my achilles tendon in half, and was in a moon boot for eight weeks, and found it hard to get to work. I enjoyed my time at home, and decided I'd rather stay at home and just walk away, rather than to continue being bullied.

During this time, my sister Kelly and I decided we would start another business together and started brokering services to vocational education companies. I told my partner I was taking over one of our offices, and we hired the room out for community services courses. As with any start-up, we didn't make much in the beginning, but it was enough to get me fired up, to walk back into my business, and demand to either be bought out, buy my partner out, or sell the business and both walk away. Unfortunately, nothing was resolved, until my partner told me she had cancer, and I had to take the company back. She passed away within a few weeks. Despite our issues, I had a hard time coming to terms with her death, and was devastated for her children.

Being thrown back in the deep end for the first time in four years, I had access to our accounts. However, what I found almost broke me. We owed the tax office hundreds of thousands of dollars, superannuation had not been paid, and clients had been stolen and put through a secret company. During this time, I had also racked up about $30,000 in credit card debt paying my home loan, car loan and general living expenses. The small amount coming in from my new business with my sister was also cut short when a training company that owed us a significant amount of money went under.

I was at a huge crossroads. Staff and clients had started coming back once they'd heard I was back and in charge. But how would I ever be able to pay off the debts? I sought accounting advice, and negotiated payment plans with the tax office. All advice pointed towards closing the business, going bankrupt, and negotiating a reduced rate with the Tax Office. However, this didn't sit well with me. As much as I felt cheated and lied to, I knew it was my responsibility to step up and make things right. I didn't want to put 20 staff off, or have them miss out on the super they were owed. I didn't want vulnerable clients to be left without care. The same factors that made me buy the company in the first place were the exact reasons why I had to keep fighting! I knew I could turn the company around, and I had the best support team in my corner!

I called all of our staff, I called all of our clients, and I told them what was going on. If I was going to do this, I needed to be honest with everyone. I had no money for payroll, or bills. But what I did find was a heap of debtors that I hounded and brought in as much cash as I could in a very short time. I took each day at a time. Then each week, then each month. Each fortnight, we just made payroll. We would cut it fine, and I did the best balancing act with our bills, but every fortnight, right on the death knock when I thought we were done, debtors would pay just enough to make payroll. I always pictured enough money in the bank!

Slowly I paid off the super debts. Slowly I paid off the two company cars. Slowly I paid the tax debt down as best I could. But I still had more hard decisions to make. I needed to reduce our personal debts so I could invest back into the company, so we sold my husband's car. Then we had to make the hard decision, to sell our house. But we had nowhere to go. Again, at the last minute, an opportunity came up to move into my Nan's house. Saved by the bell once again!

I needed to get more experience and knowledge on how to run a company solo. I had to take over every aspect of the business, including the accounts which I previously had no access to. The business was gaining more and more traction. We were getting more and more clients, some old ones coming back, and new ones coming on. I attended as many free events as I could. Yes I was a freeple! But those events gave me just enough to be able to grow more. Then I could attend cheap events. Then I could buy $1000/hour coaching!

Everything seemed to be ticking along when the unexpected happened... I fell pregnant. To say we were over the moon is an understatement. We had been trying for several years, but the biggest factor in it finally happening, was getting sober. Christian had gotten sober on our honeymoon, and I had stopped for a few months to support him.

However, after five or six months, I decided I never really had a problem, and decided to get extremely drunk for my sister's birthday. It was then that I realised that I was now drinking for other people, and that I finally believed I could give up drinking for good. Ironically, on my seven year anniversary of becoming sober... this book is launching on Amazon! Getting sober was very much the best thing I have ever done. I had tried many times before, but one thing I learnt, is to never give up giving up! Keep trying! It does stick eventually! Without sobriety I strongly doubt I would have my marriage, my business, or my son, Austin.

My pregnancy was long and tedious, riddled with issues. After a 10-hour labour, I was finally rushed in for an emergency c-section. Not long after finding out I was pregnant, fear set in. I knew the worst of the kind of world I was bringing my baby into. I had evidence of that, with not only my own trauma, but also the traumas I see with my clients every day, the brutal murder of a close family member, I see disconnection, addiction, mental health, homelessness, abuse... all in a day's work. So it was little wonder that due to my own trauma, I was more susceptible to Post Natal Depression.

Some days though, the worst thing about being a counsellor, about being a mental health professional, is that while you are pointing out everyone else's mentally ill health issues, you can be totally oblivious to your own until it's too late.

Austin was born premature at 46 weeks, after I had been in the hospital for eight weeks with pre-eclampsia. He was whisked off straight after he was born, and I was sent to recovery for several hours. My husband went with the baby, and had no idea if I was alive. Luckily several hours later, after a lot of yelling, he was allowed to come and find me.

I finally met our baby at 3:30am, when he was brought in for his first attempt at feeding. I have never been so scared in my life than I was at that moment. There was no flood of love, it was all fear. Of course love came as soon as I looked in his eyes, but the fear never went away. My husband was asleep in a corner, and I was alone looking down at this creature that I had no idea how to look after or how to keep safe.

A few days later we took him home, and if I thought it was hard in the hospital, I had no idea what I was in for at home. He barely slept. Ever. I tried to dose when he dosed, but I was also still trying to run a company! Who did I think I was? Either choose to be a Mum or a CEO! Never! I wanted it all.

After weeks and eventually months of severe sleep deprivation, I was not only deathly unhappy, I was overwhelmed with the business and the baby. I managed to fool everyone, and people assumed that because I was used to noticing mental health issues in others, that I was obviously totally fine. But I wasn't even close! I began being so unhappy and isolated, that when I got overwhelmed, I would have a bath, and I would shave my legs, and then push the razor into my skin as hard as I could. I wasn't exactly cutting myself, but I was digging the shaver in as hard as I could.

When every book, magazine, T.V show and online forum jokes about Mum's living on wine, I finally understood why. It was the hardest job in the world… and I couldn't have wine! I'd been sober several years at this point, so drinking wasn't an option. I knew that parenthood was going to be the single biggest threat to my sobriety than anything else. I managed to keep my head just above water, until it happened… the Tax Office garnished all of my bank accounts. I hadn't quite finished paying off all of the tax debt, and because we were still trading, I was also racking up more tax debt, as you do when you're running a company. I'd gone to pay a bill, and realised the accounts were empty. Every single cent was gone. All of the money I'd been managing like a well-oiled machine… Gone.

I was home alone with the baby, and I was a mess. 'That's it, we are done!' I thought. My mind was racing. How was I going to pay next week's payroll? How would I pay rent? How would we live? How would my staff live? I couldn't put 35 people off work. What about the clients? We can't organise another company to take them on so that they can get out of bed, or get their medication, etc. I ran to the bathroom and threw up. I was done. I was a failure. My mind raced around and around. How could I face anyone? My husband and sister would be out of work too, as they both worked for me. We don't even have another wage to fall back on. My mind was racing at a million miles an hour. I texted my husband. I texted my sister. 'We are done, it's happened, we have nothing left.'

They were encouraging and said we could sort it out, but I couldn't see it. I was crying, I was throwing up. I looked at my son. He was in the play pen in the lounge room. He looked at me, and I knew in that moment I had to die. I couldn't let my son grow up to find out what a failure I was or how I'd ruined so many lives. I was hysterical. My insurance money would cover most of the debt. If I died, the debt could be covered, and everyone would be ok. It was the only way out that I could see.

I picked up my baby and I said goodbye, I smelled his beautiful head, and I took eight Endones. The hospital had given them to me after the c-section, but I didn't like that they knocked me out, and I couldn't function for my son. Now, that was exactly what I wanted. I put my baby back in the play pen, I texted my husband and sister to say goodbye, and I layed down on the couch to fade away. Everything I'd been through flooded through my mind, and I was relieved I could finally be free...that I would finally be at peace. I closed my eyes and nodded off.

"Wake up!" I woke up with a gasp. My husband was slapping me across the face. My son was crying. I couldn't lift my head off the cushion. I had wet myself, and was lying in a pool of drool. This... this right here, was rock bottom. I was so useless that I couldn't even kill myself properly! Christian was yelling at me, and trying to sooth the baby. I couldn't talk. My face was numb. All I could do was drool. "I'm calling an ambulance!" Christian was still yelling and crying and had put the baby down. I was trying to shake my head. I'd worked in Social Services long enough to know that if he called the ambulance, there would be questions asked, I'd be committed, and they would take my baby. Christian was holding me now, and I was shaking my head saying 'No' as best I could. "They'll take the baby", I tried to say. Christian was in too much shock, and still hadn't called the ambulance. As I started to come around properly, I kept saying that they would take the baby if they came. He agreed not to call unless I got worse. Luckily I didn't. It took me a long time to come around, and a lot of it is a blur, but as far as defining moments go, this was easily my biggest. Of all the things I'd been through, the Tax Office emptying my accounts was the thing that pushed me over the edge. It wasn't because of the money; that meant very little. It was feeling like a failure and that I'd let everyone down.

I knew then that I needed help, and that all of the healing I thought I had done was just scratching the surface. It took many months to get back on my feet, both mentally, and financially. Some hard conversations, difficult decisions, and finally I could do what I should have done my whole life... I asked for help. I was honest with my tribe. But most importantly, I was honest with myself. Honest that my mental health had declined. Honest that sleep deprivation, running a company, trying to be everything to everyone, was running me into the ground. Honest that I was lonely and isolated, and I needed my family. I needed people around me who could help.

So we made the decision to move back to my home town where I had people to help. I made the decision to take stock, to breathe, and to take myself out of the day to day running of my business. I made the decision that I don't have to be super woman. I don't have to be super mum and super business woman. I made the decision to stop working hard and to start working smart. I finally realised I had to be completely vulnerable, completely raw, and completely honest, so that I could build my way back from the gutter. From the depths. I had to hit rock bottom before I could rebuild my foundations. I had to embrace support, and give up being a victim. I had to empower myself. I had to find new ways to function. I had to live, for my son, for my husband, for my family. I have to be around to prove that I am not a failure.

So I rebuilt. From the ground up. I stepped back, I wrote a list of the things I needed to do to get well. I needed to do what I knew would make me proud of myself. I needed to help more people without ruining me in the process. I enrolled to become a counsellor so I could work with other survivors of sexual abuse, so I could work with other mums with post natal depression, and so I could heal myself through helping others.

That was three years ago. It feels like a lifetime. Two of my companies are bigger, better, stronger and more prosperous than they have ever been. I now spend more time planning what I really want...what my real soul purpose is.

Then an idea... a lightbulb moment... original thought. A new venture. Combining all of the things I love. One that has the power to help thousands of people. One that will empower people with disabilities to live independently. One that will empower hundreds of young people living in nursing homes to be able to get out. One that will financially empower every day investors. One that will be my legacy to the world.

But this time, I was to do what I had never done before... ask for help!

"When you hit
rock bottom the
only way to go
is up."

~ Unknown

CHAPTER FIVE

When the Heart Hits Rock Bottom

By Tom Baron

"**R**ock Bottom"... I think we all probably have our own idea or life experience that defines what it means to each of us. For me, it was a broken heart, when everything I believed about love was shattered! First I'll need to unravel my life a bit for you, so you can see where my beliefs in love and how life is supposed to go, were developed.

I grew up the youngest of three kids. I have two older sisters, with Cindy being the eldest and Audrey in the middle. We are all three years apart in age. I'm the cutest and sweetest of the three of us by far!

I was born in 1964, so my formidable years really began in the early 70s. Family was everything back then! My father worked for Detroit Edison and was already up and gone to work by the time we kids would have to be up for school. My mother was the typical housewife of that time and was quite impressive with how she ran the household with what seemed like such ease! Of course, since I was such an angel of a kid, it made it that much easier for her. Mom would make sure we all got up, had breakfast, and then got off to school on time. Evenings typically consisted of dinner on the table when dad got home, and we would all sit down and eat together, followed by dad eventually falling asleep in his recliner and snoring loudly. Of course he would say, "I don't snore". This then became a mission for us kids to prove that he did. Now, dad working for the electric company had some pretty cool perks. Our family was able to get some of the latest technology that other families were not. One of those cool things was a compact tape recorder, and by compact, I mean it was the size of a shoe box. We managed to sneak it under his chair and record his bellowing snore fest! Win for the kids!

On Sundays we went to church in the morning. Mom and Dad are very strong in their Catholic beliefs; I'll write more on that later. After church, we would come home and Mom would cook up the Sunday dinner, then from there we would move on to family gatherings at my Grandma and Grandpa Baron's with all the aunts, uncles and cousins. Then we would head to Mom's side to visit Grandma Dipple and Uncle Larry who lived with and took care of my Grandma. All the cousins would fill the tiny living room to watch "The Wonderful World of Disney" movie together to finish off the night. Holidays were never-ending with daily trips to a different family member's house to visit. Just about everything we did was centered around family, and I loved it! So my beliefs were formed. Get married, have kids, raise them and watch them do the same, and spend time together enjoying each other!

I never really saw my mom and dad fight. I mean, they had their disagreements... what married couple doesn't, right? But they are very private people, so if there was a major disagreement or personal situation that needed handling, then it was handled in private and I was none the wiser about it. What I did see on a daily basis however, was what love and respect looked like in a marriage and I knew that is what I would have for myself when it was my turn. I would be a good and loving husband and father like my dad is, and I'd marry a girl who would want the same things in life for our family. Great things to strive for as a kid in the 70s right?

Then came the 80s....wow! The dreaded teenage years! Those who currently know me might never believe this, but I was a bit of a shy teenager. I wasn't the "chick magnet" that I am today, you know (wink wink). I guess what I struggled with the most was maintaining my virtues and beliefs in a world that was so rapidly changing around me, and I was terrified to change with it. It's not what I grew up knowing. I didn't really date because I was looking for the right girl that would fit my beliefs in what I thought a relationship should look like.

Let me back track a bit. I went to a Catholic school through eighth grade. When I entered the public high school, because of where we lived in the city, I was the only kid from my class going to this school. In ninth grade, I went to a new school where the only people I knew were my neighbor friend down the street and my sister, who doesn't count (and I mean that in a loving way). So yeah, I was scared and awkward to say the least. There were cliques back then, just as there are now. We had three cliques: the Jocks, which was anyone in sports or cheer, the Burnouts, who just wanted to party and get high, and last but not least, the Nerds, which consisted of pretty much everyone else. I didn't really fit into any of those categories. I played football in eighth grade and liked it (and was even pretty good at it!), but the city didn't pass their local school millage that year, so there was no football to join my freshman year, so the Jocks were out. I had only really gotten high once or twice before ninth grade, so I didn't fit in with the Burnouts, and there was just no freaking way I was going to be a Nerd!!

I met my "first love", Sue, in gym class on the tennis courts. The gym teacher paired us up and it was hate at first sight. Well, she hated me at least, because I would hit the tennis ball as hard as I could like a baseball, out of the caged-in courts every chance I got. Now, I wasn't thinking that this is someone I wanted to date at first, so I didn't really care if she liked me or not; I just really didn't want to play tennis and figured the gym teacher would switch me to something else. WRONG! I said to myself, "Tennis it is, so make the best of it". That turned into "Hey, this girl is pretty cute and now we're actually having fun with this". And that's how it all started. Sue is two years older than me, and we dated my whole way through high school. I knew what I knew from mom and dad about relationships, but for all practical purposes, I didn't know squat. So there I was, 14 years old, didn't even have a driver's license yet, dating "an older woman" who had to drive us everywhere. We dated throughout high school and even considered the "M word!" In that time, I started to develop some lifelong relationships with her family. Sue was a major part of me becoming who I am because she was my first for so many things. First love, first lover, and first heartbreak! During this time period, my sister Cindy was also in a serious relationship with Mark, the man who would become her husband and the father of my niece and nephew. My sister Audrey was not in any real serious relationship yet but change was coming for all of us!

Sue and I ended up going our separate ways, although like I said earlier, I remained great friends with her entire family, even to this day. Cindy was now married and had two kids and with Mark, Audrey was married to Tim and she now had two kids as well, but her marriage was troubled and failing. I remember feeling so torn inside because Tim was useless as a husband and father and thinking that this is who she's stuck with for the rest of her life was hard! Again, with my upbringing and mom and dad's example, the words divorce didn't even enter into my thoughts, but divorce is exactly what ended up happening for Audrey and thus, another crack in my belief system.

Debi was my second true love and future wife. Debi and I met when I was in my early 20s. This was a few years after Sue and I had split up. In between, I dated a bit, but I wasn't really into it. I will say that by the end of my relationship with Sue and because of the circumstances of our breakup, I started developing trust issues, so not getting emotionally attached to someone became quite easy. Anyway, something about Debi broke through that barrier. I found myself falling in love pretty quickly. She was quiet but we had a very good relationship and communicated well together, at least at first we did! We got married in 1989, and in 1991, our beautiful baby girl Brittany was born. In the two years in between, Debi and I did quite a bit of partying. Back then, weed, alcohol, and cocaine were the party favors of choice, and we did our fair share. We knew that once we got serious about building the family, we would have to put that partying away (or at least I did!). Everything was working out for me pretty much like I thought it should in marriage, but you don't know what you don't know.

I remember how excited Debi was when we found out she was pregnant. She had "the glow"! She was such a happy expecting mother and I was a proud soon-to-be daddy! Then came the 4:00am "Honey, I think my water just broke" wake-up nudge, and off to the hospital we went. This was a bit concerning since we were six weeks out from her due date, but "it's all going to be fine" I thought. As the labor dragged on, they decided to add a fetal heart monitor to the scene and, of course, this wigged me out a bit because every time Debi would have a contraction, the baby's heart rate would dive. When we were at nearly 24 hours of labor, they finally decided it was time to get that baby out, so off we went for an emergency C-section! Everything was happening so freaking fast. Within minutes of entering the operating room, I heard Brittany's very first cry and my heart was forever changed. She weighed in at a whopping five pounds six ounces and was a mere 17" long, but she was perfect in my eyes! I remember when they handed her to me, and I just kept envisioning what our future together looked like. One of my most cherished memories was bringing Brittany home and having our first night together, just the two of us. Debi had to stay in the hospital an extra day because she had a slight fever. All the women in my life at the time wanted to come over and help me that first night, but I said, "Nope, thanks, but I got this"! And I did. I was prepared! I had a good job that gave me the means to provide for my family, I had a loving wife who just gave me the most precious gift ever, and I was able to spend that very first night with her with absolute confidence! All my ducks were lining up, and things were going just as they were supposed to go...at least, so I thought.

It didn't take too long to realize that things actually weren't right. I worked a swing shift at a drywall manufacturing plant and put in quite long hours. I would work seven straight days on one shift until getting one or two days off, and then switching to the next shift for seven days, and so on. I was home for the first week or so while Debi recovered from the C-section, but then it was back to work and time to do my part as a husband and father. I would get home and Brittany would be in her play pen and Debi would be, for lack of a better word, useless. I would pick up Brittany and hold her, feed her, and bathe her while Debi became more and more distant from us. At first, I chalked it up to her just being tired and having a hard time bouncing back from surgery; but as time went on, it became more and more obvious that things were just not right and my ideal "family life" wasn't materializing the way it was supposed to. It was disintegrating before my very eyes, even through the rose colored glasses I had chosen to wear kept me believing this was just a phase. That was until other people started questioning her behavior and I was forced to face reality.

Denial sucks! Sometimes we spend all of our time hiding away from what we know in our hearts is true because we're just terrified to accept it. Well, sooner or later, reality walks right up and smacks you in the face and there's no denying it anymore. For me, that reality came when I went to purchase something and was told I had insufficient funds in my account. "WAIT, WHAT!?" How is this even possible with the money that we make together?" "This must be a mistake!" Now, my mom was the one who handled all the finances in our household and she was incredible at it. Debi ran the office at her dad's business, so having her handle the bills for our family was only natural, so I didn't need to worry! Well, I started doing a little investigating, and what I found out sent me into a downward spiral that took me to a place I never want to see again!

Accounts were overdrawn, bills were late and just totally being ignored. We didn't have cell phones and computers to give up to the minute information on your finances like we do now. Everything was based on a trust that the right thing was being done. So where was all the money going? She wasn't buying stuff for Brittany, herself, or for the house, so where was it going? Then came the night when we were out with our friends (my former girlfriend Sue's family) celebrating a birthday, and I caught her with a couple grams of cocaine. Yep, that's $200 dollars that she was planning on blowing right up her nose and right under mine! "How can you do this?" I wondered. "Is this why you seem uninterested in me and Brittany?" After the confrontation, I tried to believe her...that it was just a one time thing, she was sorry, and that it would never happen again. I so wanted to believe that to be true. I mean, after all, she knows now that I am watching our money and she won't be able to get away with that again, right? WRONG!

Remember what I said about denial? It sucks! Things weren't getting better; in fact, they continued to worsen. The distance between us widened further and further. I didn't want to believe what was happening, which made it easier for her to take this to the next level. Since she couldn't take our money any longer, she would need to come up with another way to feed her addiction. It started with late nights at the office and then she would go out on the weekends for hours at a time. This may not seem like that big of a deal, but it just wasn't something she would have done normally, so the red flags started going up! Yes, denial! I knew what was happening but didn't want to face it. This didn't fit in with what I was brought up to believe about relationships and marriage, so instead of facing it, I turned to more destructive behaviors myself. Two can play at this game, right? I could drink and get high with the best of them, and I did. We tell ourselves that we do what we do to dull the pain, and there was so much pain in my heart! "How could this be happening?" I learned from the best on how love and a good marriage should look and feel, so, what the hell was I doing wrong? Yes, self-blame takes hold in a big way!

It all came to a head one Friday morning when she said she was going to visit a friend for the weekend and was taking our daughter with her. No big deal right? Then I asked her for the phone number of her friend in case I would need to get in touch with her. (Remember, no cell phones back then, only land lines.) "Why do you need that?" she asked. "Don't you trust me?" Ummm, NO!, I thought to myself. I asked her, "Why would you even hesitate to give me a number of where you're going to be with our daughter?" After some back and forth I finally said, "Why won't you just admit that you're having an affair?" And she did! That is the exact moment my heart hit rock bottom! I couldn't deny it any longer. I was devastated on the inside, but my defense mechanism took over, and a calm, clear picture of what I needed to do immediately appeared in my head. First I told her, "Hand me my daughter", and then I went and put her in her play pen in the other room. I then calmly told her to gather whatever she needed and said, "Don't say anything...just get out." Later, I discovered that she was having an affair with a coworker and, of course, he was providing her with all the cocaine she wanted!

Immediately after she left, I grabbed the phone book and looked for a lawyer. The first name I saw was a local female lawyer. I called and said, "I want to file for divorce and custody of my daughter today!" They told me to come in as soon as possible and they would talk to me. Next, I was off to the bank. We had just gotten a joint credit card that had never been used, so I took out a cash advance for the entire line of credit. I then went to see the lawyer. As I sat there waiting on the lawyer to come in, I tried to sort through my emotions. I was feeling things that I had never felt before. I guess the biggest was "fear of the unknown". I thought, "I'm going to be a single father. What have we done to our daughter's life? What is that going to look like now? Is Debi going to fight me for custody?" I was getting paranoid inside! Then, in walked the lawyer. She was a tall, slender, incredibly attractive woman, and immediately a calm fell over me. I thought to myself, "If I have a lawyer that looks like her on my side, I've got it made!" I know it sounds bad on my part, but at the time, my thought process was a bit skewed, so let's just go with that.

I left the lawyer's office with her paid in full and a filing for divorce and sole custody being delivered to the judge that same afternoon. My next stop was the hardware store to buy some new locks for the doors, which were changed the minute I returned home. Now for the really hard part...telling Mom and Dad. Three kids and now three failed marriages, all ending in divorce. Yes, three, because by this time, Cindy's marriage had ended in a similar fashion with drugs and infidelity by her husband. How do I tell them? This is just going to crush them! Ours was going to be the marriage that lasted! Well, it turns out that parents are pretty darn smart and they knew that things were going south for us, so it really didn't come as a big surprise to them. They saw the signs that I had done my best to cover up. Sure, they were saddened, but more than anything, they were supportive and that's what I desperately needed.

It's been said that I can be pretty intimidating at times, and I suppose that must be true to some extent because I absolutely intimidated Debi into to believing she was followed by a private detective and that everything she had been doing would be brought out in court if she even *thinks* about fighting me for custody! The intimidation worked because she didn't fight me one bit; however, it also turned out that she never planned to. She didn't want custody. "WHAT???" What kind of mother doesn't fight for her child? She wanted to do her thing with her new lover, who, by the way, was also married and had three kids, and he devastated his family as well. He would later take his own life! So sad for his innocent children. This was all prior to our divorce being finalized. So, can you guess what happened next? That's right...I got the, "I'm so sorry, I really screwed up...can we please give it one more try?" phone call.

My dilemma was this: If I said no, then for the rest of my life, I would wonder and feel guilty that I didn't try for the sake of our daughter. She was the innocent one in all of this. I had to at least try for her, I thought, so after much talking, I agreed to put the brakes on and give it another chance. This was very short-lived and ultimately the divorce was back on and finalized with me having sole legal and joint physical custody of Brittany. Debi basically had visitation rights. I was now a single dad, raising his daughter alone, and I was good with that! My heart was so damaged from this that I had absolutely no desire to have another woman in my life again! It was me and Brittany against the world, and we were doing just fine on our own. Or were we?

Once a month I would get a long weekend off from work and Brittany and I would almost always take a two-hour drive to spend the weekend at my closest friend's home. At the time, it was the one true place that I felt happy. We always had so much fun and I could escape the pain in my heart that I just couldn't seem to shake otherwise. I remember this like it was yesterday. It was a gorgeous summer morning and we were out in the Florida room of their house having our morning coffee when Maryanne asked the question, "So Tom, when are you going to start dating?" Without thought, the word "NEVER" came shooting out my mouth. She looked at me and said, "You're just not the kind of guy who is meant to be alone", and although I didn't acknowledge it at the time, she was absolutely right. I had worked extremely hard building a wall around my heart, and just like that, a crack appeared. I hated being alone, but I wouldn't ever allow someone to hurt me like that ever again. Not to mention, I had a daughter to protect as well. I would soon find out that Brittany would face challenges far beyond a broken family as a result of our failed marriage.

Brittany was developing much slower than other kids her age. Maybe it was the fact that I was a single dad and she was my first child, so everything was new. Or maybe it was denial again. Or perhaps it was a little of both, but I didn't really see it. After some urging from family and friends, I decided to start the process of unraveling what was going on with her. At this point, she was my only concern and I had no time to worry about anything or anyone else!

A couple years went by and, well, enter Stacey! Now, remember how I told you that I had developed incredible friendships with Sue's family? Well, I was attending a wedding for one of the family, and that's when Stacey and I first officially met. I say "officially" because we would later recall that we probably met years before. Ready for a plot twist? Stacey is Sue's cousin!

I was working a 3:00am to 3:00pm shift, so there was no drinking for me that night, but standing by the bar is the best place to mingle since everyone stops by sooner or later. Sue's brother and I were talking when I noticed this rather cute girl that I'd never met before heading toward us. She gave my buddy a big hug and he then introduced us. We all hung out there for the night and had an awesome time. Although we hit it off and enjoyed each other's company, she was married and I was wrapped up in my own things, dealing with Brittany and her issues. But man, there was something about this girl that cracked that wall around my heart a little bit wider. Then came another family wedding that we were both at, and this time she was there but she was with her dad, not her husband. As I would find out later, their marriage was on the downward spiral. We had talked again and had an amazing time together and, just like that, the wall was gone.

We spent that night talking, laughing, dancing, and getting to know each other. She had a son who was just a year old and a marriage that was falling apart. I could totally relate, and we connected more because of my history of going through a similar situation. I remember dancing with her and these words just blurted out of my mouth, "I want to have another baby!" The fact that she didn't just walk away from me right there was a plus! Instead, she said, "I do too!" and I started to feel something I hadn't in quite a long time. But wait, she's still married and she lives in another state for God's sake...what are you thinking man? That night ended and reality took over again. I had to take care of my daughter first and foremost.

Did you ever hear the saying, "The heart wants what the heart wants"? Well, it's a true statement; at least it was in my world at that time. I could not stop thinking of Stacey and wondered when I would see her again. That opportunity came when Stacey's cousin Sue called her and asked her to come into town for the annual Fourth of July fireworks show on the Detroit River. "We'll sail down on the boat and Tom will be there" she told her, and Stacey agreed to come! I was absolutely thrilled that we would see each other again!

We fell in love on the boat that night, with fireworks literally right over our heads. It was pure magic! We just didn't know exactly how to go forward with it, for obvious reasons. Then came the annual family camping trip and again, Sue bugged Stacey to come. She told Sue that she was afraid to because she was technically still married, but she wanted to see me as much as I wanted to see her! She ended up coming for the first weekend and then came back the following weekend, and that is when I was be introduced to my future son, Philip. It was full steam ahead after that first weekend camping. This incredible girl completely tore down that wall around my heart and had me feeling things that I never ever felt before.

For the next year and a half, we carried on a long-distance relationship and it was like a romance novel when we would be together and countless hours on the phone when we were apart. My long distance phone bill was more than most people's mortgages, but I didn't care! We would talk about our hopes and dreams, the challenges we were facing with our kids, ex's, and just everyday life. We would just talk and it was amazing.

By this time, I had already been divorced and on my own with Brittany for three years, but for her, everything was new and still fresh from her divorce. She started to feel nervous and questioning herself if she was rushing things, and I didn't make matters better since I had a handful of things that happened in a row that would make the hair on most people's neck stand up. Bad luck to say the least. She told me she wanted to have time to possibly date other people to know for sure if we were right. I felt like I was hit by a bus! I told myself, "You see? This is what happens! You aren't meant to be with anyone!" I was pretty devastated. I felt that wall starting to build back up and I just hated that feeling! Then one night I was sitting alone in my apartment feeling lost and confused and a commercial came on the TV for a psychic. Trust me, I know what you're thinking. I couldn't believe I was actually dialing the number myself, but I was desperate to know something, even if it wasn't what I wanted to hear. Well, it was actually everything I wanted to hear! We were going to get married and we were going to have a child together and it would happen much sooner than I thought. I told her that I called a psychic and what the psychic said, and that I really wanted to see her just to talk things through and she cautiously agreed. I still had a key to her home and I let myself in, which happened to be right before she got home from work. As she will recall, I was standing there looking out the back sliding glass door, when I heard her letting herself in. As she will tell you, the sun beams were shining around me like a mystical being, and when we looked at each other, we instantly knew we were meant to be together, come thick or thin; needless to say, the magic in our relationship was back and in full force.

Fast forward one full year, things were going great between us both and neither of us wanted anything other than to be together, so I planned a romantic night together to propose to her and make things official. We had a magical engagement night with dinner, dancing, and romance. Going forward, we had to figure out many details in order for this to work. With Stacey in Pittsburgh and I in Detroit, this meant someone is going to have to move, and we also had the ex-spouses to deal with. Long story short, we determined that our best bet was for me to move to Pittsburgh and the plan was set into motion.

During all of this, I was still struggling to find answers about Brittany's developmental delays. For months, I had been getting the runaround from her pediatrician telling me she was just small and she needs growth hormones, but that wasn't acceptable to me. She wasn't answering my question. I wanted to know "Why"... Why is she so small? Why is she so far behind kids her age? Why, why, why? She was finally tested at Children's Hospital in Ann Arbor, Michigan by the genetics team. That call came the day before I was to be married and the message I was told was, "Your daughter has a chromosome disorder causing her to face severe developmental delays and learning disabilities, and there is no cure." I was devastated!! A million thoughts raced through my head as you can imagine, and then it hit me, "You're supposed to be getting married tomorrow!" I had to tell Stacey. How will she react to this? Will she want to call off the wedding and run for the hills? Well, thank God for both of us that she didn't! That should give you an indication of just what an amazing woman she is!

So, this is how our wedding day went: We met on the Ohio Turnpike early that morning, her coming from Pennsylvania and me from Michigan, and we drove to Toledo together, just the two of us, to be married in a courthouse hallway by a justice of the peace. From there, we went and had wedding day lunch at a nice, local restaurant that we found by driving around the small city. Then it was back to Michigan where we rented a moving van and loaded all of Brittany's and my things, and off to our new life in Pittsburgh. I even received a lovely wedding gift from an Ohio State Trooper in the form of a $125 speeding ticket! (This still pisses me off to this day!) Oh and I almost forgot...Stacey was starting a brand new job the very next day!

Now, anyone that is in a blended family knows that the struggles of "your kid" and "my kid" are very real, and we were no exception. The birth of our daughter Kate completed the, "yours, mine and ours" family dynamics for us. All three kids are so incredibly different and unique, all three beautiful, loving souls in their own ways. Sure, we've had our share of tough times as a couple and a family, and some pretty dark times early on, but we will continue to get through whatever comes our way.

The heart is a strong muscle, folks. It can endure so much more than we think. I'm writing this to give hope to someone who might be hurting inside, wanting to give up, and thinking that it's never going to get better than this! Don't believe those self-limiting lies, because that's what they are, lies! I found the love of my life, my soulmate, my "FOREVER", and I wasn't even looking. You can too! Maybe these words can help put a crack in the wall you've built around your heart. I sure hope so, because you are worth it!

"Accept - then act. Whatever the present moment contains, accept it as if you had chosen it. This will miraculously transform your whole life."

~ Eckhart Tolle

CHAPTER SIX

Mastering Midlife

By Suzie Martin Huening

Life is pretty good. I must admit, I had it good growing up. Not to the extent I was spoiled, well not in the "brat" kind of way at least, and not because my family was super wealthy, but we were doing okay financially. There were times when my mom was a single mother and we didn't have as much, so I always had gratitude for all the things in my life. I always felt like I had options. Sure, I came from a "broken home", but that wasn't too uncommon, although it's far more common now.

In high school, I was a cheerleader, on the homecoming court, and was modeling. In my senior year, I was even offered a few modeling contracts in New York City with well-known agencies. I was only 17 years old, so the decision wasn't entirely up to me, but I opted for college, in spite of the agencies warning me "Your education can wait, your age can't! Models are washed up by 22 years old these days."

Yeah, well...I'll be "washed up" with a degree, I thought. I wanted to join my friends in college. I had always seen myself going off to college, having fun, and was excited about that upcoming chapter in my life. I was flattered to be offered that opportunity, but scared of going it alone up in NYC. I heard all the models were hooked on cocaine, had eating disorders, and were sleeping their way to the top. I was not a city girl, and that was one busy city; I was intimidated, and boy was it expensive! While they spoke of six figures per year contracts, my mom assured me that wouldn't be much up in that city. I think she was leveraging her parental influence without telling me she didn't want me to go. It worked.

College was a great experience. I have no regrets. I still managed to do quite a bit of modeling, was in two movies, several commercials, played the lead in a music video by one of my favorite East Coast bands, and only graduated one semester behind, on the Dean's List. During college, I also started working out at a health club, teaching aerobics and ultimately competing in bodybuilding contests. In spite of not being very big muscularly, I did well with my lean, lanky build. I loved exercising! This ignited my lifelong passion for health and fitness. But, I graduated with a bachelors degree in fine art/graphic design. Now, this was back in the 1980s, when graphic design was done by hand, not a computer. Shortly after I graduated, I moved to Sarasota, Florida after falling in love with the place when I helped my mom and step-dad move. I started my job search only to find that places were only hiring for paste up, which required absolutely no education, and only paid minimum wage. Then, to add insult to injury, graphic design went to computers. So I opted to work in health clubs and restaurants, just like I did in college.

It was in a health club where I met my first husband. He was the manager, and we were not supposed to be dating. At the the time, he was very charming and into bodybuilding like I was. But, our short courtship was surprised by an unexpected pregnancy. I suddenly started feeling those "options" that I had always had disappear. I had been stuck working in a gym, and now I was pregnant and getting married. However, after the initial shock, I was beyond excited to have my baby. And once I had him and saw his face, my whole universe shifted. I felt a power surge within me that I had never felt. It was the purist feeling of love I had ever experienced. I felt...no...I KNEW, that I would do anything for my baby.

Unfortunately, 'doing anything' meant allowing myself to be treated with no respect from my husband. Over time, he became increasingly more verbally abusive, which started turning to physical abuse. I guess I'm lucky that he never punched me. What he did do was bad enough; shoved me hard enough to send me flying backwards, choked me until I nearly passed out, rammed his forehead into mine, while pinning my head to a wall...as he yelled at me enraged with veins bulging in his face and neck and spit shooting out of his mouth. It didn't help that it was rumored he was on steroids, and I'm pretty certain that was the case. But I was in survival mode. I had a child and my income was dependent on our health club that we co-owned with an investor. We had a lovely home and it would just be so much easier to make it work. He kept telling me he wasn't happy and didn't know why, so his mother paid for him to go to a psychiatrist, thinking he had a chemical imbalance. He came home from that appointment laughing. He told me that the psychiatrist told him he had Narcissistic Personality Disorder, and that there was really nothing he could do because they usually don't see that they are the ones needing to change. And, in fact, that it's usually the people who are in relationships with them that would benefit from the therapy. He smugly said, "So I guess you're the one who needs the help, not me."

During this high-stress time, I had been dealing with severe bouts of my knees swelling, coupled with debilitating pain. My knees would look unrecognizable. Again, my husband would just laugh at my pain and tell me it was psychosomatic. After, nearly seven years and a few brief separations initiated by him, we split for good. He told me, once again, he wasn't happy; however, this time he did say it wasn't me...that I was wonderful, he just wasn't happy. I had some serious suspicions that he was having an affair with my friend, who was also our employee. I didn't want to believe it. It was too painful to believe that two people I cared for thought so little of me, that they would both betray me. But I would be in my office with a sick pit in my stomach as I watched their office lines staying lit up simultaneously for long periods and both lights going out at the same time. It happened far too frequently to be a coincidence. Then there were times when she would pick up my son from school, then a kindergartener, without my knowledge and take him to her house. I would show up at the school, wait in the pick-up line, only to have the teacher tell me that she had picked him up. She was a friend. Her kids went to the same school. She had permission to pick him up. I trusted her. I would arrive back at work, upset that I had adjusted appointments to pick up my son, and he wasn't there. My husband would laugh it off. She would tell me, "Just have the bossman come pick him up at my house when he leaves work. That way you don't have to go out of your way." Awwww... she was being so considerate. I knew what was happening, but I wanted to believe it wasn't true, because if I had some doubt, there just might be a chance for my family to work out in the long run. On my last day at work, I said my goodbyes to my friends who worked for us at the gym and to the members who had become my friends. Within an hour after I left, "she" moved her stuff into my old office, making her FIRST claim to what WAS once mine.

You Have More Strength and Power in Anger than you do in Despair

After a quick 45-day divorce, where I naively signed divorce papers without representation or reading them, my son and

I moved in with my mom. I made a trip back for the cats from my wild/domestic cat breeding program, which were in poor health by the time I got back, as my ex-husband hadn't cleaned the litter boxes in weeks and had barely fed them. He told me he wanted to keep our pet cat and wolf hybrid dog, only to get rid of them shortly after we moved away.

I was also able to get a few pieces of furniture, but not allowed to take anything from my son's old room, even my own artwork. My ex stood at the door, arms crossed and refused to allow me to even enter my son's old room. Basically, he kept the house, the business, and all the items in the house that he wanted to keep. He had convinced me it was all debt and he would keep the debt to help me out. I didn't realize how much equity the house and the business had. I was just hurt and humiliated. My brain wasn't working. I was weak from pain and not mad enough to fight. I felt like I was being kicked out of my own life. It was humiliating, and my self-esteem was at the lowest point in my life. He later moved my former friend and her family into my old home. As time went on and he tried to control me from afar, and I learned of all the affairs he had been having over the years, I started to become more angry than sad or hurt. Being mad is a lot better than being hurt. You have some power in anger. Being in a state victimhood leaves you weak and helpless.

At times I would have a sense of freedom and excitement about the future, and other times I felt hopeless. All my mom wanted to do was sit around and talk about how awful my ex was, and while we're at it, let's go see grandma and sit around her house and talk about how horrible her ex and my ex were. The more I spoke about it and focused on it, the worse I felt. My mom finally asked, "What can I do to make you feel better? You seem so sad all the time." I told her, "I need to be around people my own age. I need to laugh. I need to go out and go dancing. I can't keep going over to grandmas and talking about how horrible my ex was to me and my son. I need to look forward to what's ahead." She meant well, but she was mad too, that someone had hurt her baby so badly, and my mom is not one to let things go. However, she did put me in contact with a female colleague at her real estate office that was my age and usually went out in large groups for dinner, drinks, dancing, etc. I welcomed that opportunity. After all, I found out my ex had been cheating on me all along, so now it was my time to meet some cute guys. So, I'm in the lobby of the restaurant waiting to meet my party, whom I had never seen before. One cute young guy arrives in the lobby and is standing there with me. We find out we're there to meet the same group of people. He follows me around all night, and is so cute, charming and funny...oh and he can dance! That's a plus. I was ready for fun. I was due some fun. But I had no plans for a relationship.

I worked doing personal training at two gyms, and worked as a Realtor, but never made a commission. I also took on some art commissions for hand-painted furniture, which I had been doing on the side for several years. Looking back, this was actually very therapeutic. I was in the flow, creating, and listening to music. Hours would fly by without my realizing it. I felt a sense of purpose, value and accomplishment. My self esteem had taken a real hit, so feeling good about myself was welcomed. I continued to date that cute guy I met in the restaurant lobby. We had struggles. He had never been around kids much, and I was having issues with trust, but he was persistent and patient.

Nearly two years later, we were married. He was a fresh young captain in the Army, and I had no idea what it meant to be married to someone in the military, although he did try to warn me. Three years after we married, I received a call from my mom to turn on the TV. I watched in horror as the second plane hit the World Trade Center, and was glued to the news. Two stress-filled weeks later, he was deployed to an undisclosed location. I was in college to become a Physical Therapist Assistant and in the middle of my clinical rotations. That time was a like a blur. I graduated with a perfect 4.0, but my husband was deployed and missed my graduation.

There were many deployments after that initial one, mostly a few months at a time. We had decided to try to have a baby, but it just wasn't happening, so we turned to fertility treatments. After an unsuccessful IVF treatment up at Walter Reed Army Hospital, he went back to Iraq. Fortunately, we had some embryos frozen for another attempt. I was working in physical therapy, but took a few days off and went back three months after the first attempt with my mother. This time it was successful. I attached a picture of the test stick to an email (back then pictures were only attachments), and sent it to his email address downrange. I instructed him to enlarge the photo so he could appreciate what it was. He later told me that he was looking over his shoulders to make sure nobody was watching him open the photo because he thought it might have been some sort of risqué photo. Ha...I'm not the type to do that. I told him to hurry and get home because people would start talking about me if I started showing, knowing my husband wasn't around. We had a large baby boy who filled our world with joy.

I loved having a baby again, as it had been 14 years since my oldest son was born. My prayers had truly been answered. However, running my business (wild to domestic hybrid cat breeding), cleaning litter boxes, cat runs/cages, feeding my African Serval and multiple other domestic/wild hybrid cats, bottle feeding, shipping kittens, maintaining my website, as well as many other necessary tasks, and also taking care of a baby and a teenager involved in sports was stressful! I also continued to exercise, but my joints began to swell again, and I was in severe pain. My rheumatologist suggested I quit breastfeeding my baby at six months and get on disease-modifying drugs immediately. She felt I would be requiring bilateral knee replacement surgery if I didn't take immediate action. The thought scared me, so I complied. I must admit, the medication worked wonders within a couple of weeks, and I regained the quality of my life back.

When my youngest was four, we got orders to move, and my husband was already gone, so I had to handle prepping the house for the sale (repairs and painting), as well as selling the house on my own. I kept the house staged and ready to show at all times. It sold pretty quickly, but my oldest son was graduating from high school after we were to close on the sale of our house, which meant I had to get out of the house, but not the town. We all moved in with my mom temporarily until my son finished high school, and I planned his graduation party in the midst of a sudden family feud between my mom and uncle. I had broken down cat enclosures and reconstructed them on my mom's property in smaller configurations. I sold off many of my breeders so I could transport the cats to our new home. My husband would come back every couple of weeks to visit, but I managed to do most of this on my own.

We moved to our beautiful new home and I fell in love with the resort-style community. Our oldest decided to attend a university close to us instead in North Carolina. I think he really wanted to stay close to his little brother's college, and it seemed like my husband traveled overseas all the time. It was mostly just me and my sweet little boy, who was still having issues with potty training. I had no friends or family around so that I could take a break, and my husband was gone overseas quite a bit. He was gone to Germany and having fun partying after work in the beer gardens with his colleagues.

I began to sink into a dark place of resentment and loneliness. I loved my new home, but I was starting to resent my life, losing patience with potty training, and jealous of my husband traveling and having fun while I stayed behind alone, taking care of everything. I didn't feel safe, as our next door neighbor child (seven years older than my son), had some mental issues and had preyed on our little boy. I felt like I wasn't in control of my own life and I wasn't living the life I wanted...and I wasn't getting any younger. Most of all, I didn't like who I felt I was becoming. I felt guilty. I had a new beautiful home and sweet little boy to spend my days with and we were healthy and financially secure. Wasn't this what I had always wanted?

We had only been in our new home a few months when we were notified that my husband would be taking a battalion command right back at Fort Bragg, where we had just moved from. So, after being there a year, we had to move right back, but during that year, our house had lost $120K in value when the market collapsed, and we were in a panic. We decided to rent at a loss. I was not happy about leaving this beautiful home and community, and our oldest son just 20 miles down the road, only to move back to the same town we had just left. However, I took action to plan everything out like a good military spouse.

I planned ahead for housing on the other end, school registration, shots, utilities...every. little. detail. It was the one thing I thought I could control while I felt I had no control. I got to a point that I finally made an appointment with a therapist because I was anxious and depressed and felt I had no understanding or support from my husband. I knew the resentment was growing inside of me, and I felt like I had a heavy blanket of doom on me all the time. I wasn't happy.

The therapist told me I was staying in such a stressed state, trying to make sure everything was taken care of, that I had inadvertently caused a chemical imbalance by never coming "down" from this heightened state. I was feeling resentment towards my husband because he didn't seem to care what I was going through emotionally, and seemed to think it was just weakness. To me, he seemed to be far more focused on his military career than any personal meltdown I may have been having. I felt unsupported and unappreciated. However, when the therapist started to bash my husband and suggest I get on medication, something snapped in me to take charge and not feel like a victim. I took a ladies trip to the beach with some very good friends. We laughed till we cried, partied, danced all night, and laid on the beach all day. That was far more therapeutic than going to the therapist! I felt like I had hit a reboot and found my old self again. It was exactly what I needed to get rebalanced emotionally.

Since then, we've moved several more times. I'm finding an ease in not stressing myself out months ahead of time, knowing in that moment that there is nothing I can do to prepare for it. When I feel a sense of panic about all that has to be done prior to moving, I take a deep breath and remind myself that it will all work out, it always does.

Mastering Midlife

It seems like when I turned 50 years old, I started to focus more on myself again, which has helped me not to resent my husband and has improved our relationship. When I felt I was giving up everything for his career and not doing what fulfilled me, it wasn't good for either of us. It seemed he traveled the world and was always mixing fun into his work travel, and I just stayed at home taking care of STUFF. But that STUFF I focused on started to change.

By getting involved in personal development, I gained more confidence to pursue things that would normally intimidate me. So after 23 years of being on hiatus from fitness competitions, I decided to give it a go again, with the encouragement and support from my husband. I'm proud to say that I did well, and I believe that maybe I gained a little more respect from him, by him seeing me pursue something and do well. I earned my pro card in Figure at nearly 53 years old in an international, drug-tested fitness show, placed first through third in Figure and Physique shows, national qualifiers and international shows, some competing with women of all ages from many countries. Although I've been consistently working out and trying to eat a healthy diet, my health is so much better now that I'm focused more on my inner peace.

Since I have started connecting with Source through meditation, I'm in a far more peaceful state. I have love and tolerance for so much more. As I write this, I'm dealing with my mom, who was recently diagnosed with Alzheimers and who had breast cancer two years ago. I find myself observing and handling things that need to be dealt with rather than getting completely stressed out over them and letting my feelings get hurt when she lashes out at me. I know it's all part of her disease. I will admit, I could be more patient, but it's a challenge when the dynamics of a long-standing relationship completely change, and I'm still working on it. She doesn't want to be "the child" any more than I want to be "her parent", yet it often appears that that's the way it stands now, which is frustrating for both of us, at times. My brother and I are using our sense of humor to handle it as best we can. What else can we do? We have to do what is right for us and our family and not allow outside sources make us feel guilty for our decisions about our mom's care. We know that in her current condition, she's not safe to live alone. We also know that with her declining behavior, it's not something neither of us want to deal with living in our homes, especially living around our children. As unpleasant as it is, we will be placing her in a memory care center close to my brother and his family, against her will. Considering the military is moving my family a few states away in a few months, and then deploying my husband for a year to Iraq, we will make decisions that we feel will be in her, and our best interests as a family.

So here we are again, facing another military move and another deployment. I thought by now we would be done with the deployments. It is exciting to think about living on the beautiful west coast of Florida again. I'm looking forward to the white, sandy beaches and the clear, blue water. I'm looking forward to the warmer climate year round. I thrive in warm, sunny weather. I can paint outside year round. I can meditate at sunset on the beach. Yes, I'm looking forward to being in a new location. And as the to-do list builds before the move (like it always does), especially moving my mom before I move, I will continue to visualize the warm sun on my skin as I gaze at the brilliant sunset, painting the sky in hues of pink and blue and reflecting on the calm Gulf waters, while I dig my feet into the cool, white quartz sand. I am grateful for this next step. In fact, I've been visualizing it since well before my husband got orders to Tampa. I'm just regretful that he will be deployed the first year. But who knows what the Universe has in store?

"Remember that just
because you hit bottom
doesn't mean you
have to stay there."

~ Robert Downy Jr

CHAPTER SEVEN

A Journey Home

By Christian Doherty

Have you ever had those moments in life where you are doing something in particular and you are just operating on autopilot, and then you have that "What am I doing? How did I get here? There has to be something more" thought pop into your head which rocks you to your core? It's almost like you disengage from your subjective reality and gain an outside objective perspective just for a brief moment, but that brief moment shakes you loose from yourself just long enough to be able to completely alter your trajectory going forward.

I know these moments well and have had many of them, which I would say was the reason for being 35 years old, alive, clean and sober, married, a father, always actively studying, growing, expanding, and in the best shape of my life. Interestingly, I would actually say that these moments were born out of something negative. But they are the silver linings in the dark storm clouds. It reminds me of something a good friend said to me once, only recently: "Skills come from adversity." I am reminded of this time and time again.

When you are navigating difficult situations in life, you are forced to find ways to be flexible, resilient and adaptable. It's survival. Sure, sometimes the ways of surviving can have some darker aspects, but they also have silver linings. They have opportunities for growth. I spent a lot of years having my confidence and self-worth rocked by situations that were determined to take me down. Yet I survived. Only just.

I never thought I'd make it to 30 and didn't even want to, a lot of the time. I used to fantasize about a world without me in it, so that I didn't have to deal with the crushing weight of my own existence. I would be locked inside my own mind in my bedroom for days at a time, sleeping as much as I could, so I didn't have to deal with being awake with myself. The days when I wasn't locked away, I would venture out and try to feel something that wasn't pain. The upswings were very few and far between, but, in hindsight, I see that they provided the slivers of light I needed before I was swallowed completely.

Many things were the likely catalysts for this period of time; yet, if I were to go into them, it would be a book all on its own, not a chapter. So, I'll stick with the main things that led right up to this.

At 15, I was off the rails. I was involved in a very toxic relationship and was wagging school flat out. I was stealing from people and generally exhibiting a really poor attitude towards everyone. Mum and dad were at the school more than they should have been, having meetings with myself and the teachers. I promised to do better but didn't, of course. The story was always the same from teachers and had been since primary school: "Christian has so much potential and is so capable. Why is he wasting himself?" I had no idea either.

Shortly after all this was happening, I was struck down with glandular fever which did a number on me physically, emotionally, mentally, and energetically. That led to an extreme case of cystic acne all over my back, chest, face, and neck, the scars of which I still wear. Unfortunately, it was among the worst cases doctors and dermatologists had seen in their 30 years in the field. I tried EVERYTHING to help other than the major medication at the time, of which the side effects included things we were already afraid of, such as suicidal thoughts and depression. I was on antibiotics, steroid creams, herbal teas, naturopathic essences, tons of water, good food, and still I couldn't gain the relief I was seeking. It's the distinction between acne and pimples, which I learned the hard way yet still had to explain to people years later. They are completely different and not related to diet (though a good diet doesn't hurt).

Because of all of this, I was forced to take six months off from school because I couldn't stay awake, let alone focused, and was in so much pain from the acne that I couldn't stand it. It felt like my back especially was punctured with hot needles 24/7. People aren't always nice when it comes to appearance, either, so I did not want to add to my suffering any further by being the centre of attention because of my acne-riddled face. I couldn't play cricket due to not being able to be in the sun, so I essentially had nothing to do but hang out at home, watch TV, and play guitar. Those things provided pleasure in pain.

Taking six months off school meant I had to make a decision to either repeat a year or, because of my ability, the school was going to allow me to do some catch-up work and go up with my class. I considered the offers and decided to repeat a year. I think it was the better decision of the two, looking back, but, like anything, it had its positive and negative aspects. Eventually, after suffering for six years, I took the acne medication. It did cause problems, but it actually worked. It didn't help that I was drinking heavily and taking drugs while on it, which you aren't supposed to do, due to the damage it causes the liver. But I did it anyway.

That period of time taught me a lot about myself and other people. Before it, I felt as though I was a reasonably active participant in life, but during and after this time, I felt like I was more of a behind-the-scenes individual. Never wanting attention to come my way, I would just sit and observe and try to stay out of focus. Life was on hold from then on for quite a lot of time. That's how it felt. Learned helplessness was something I fell into, and the walls closed in on my world. I wasn't living, just existing.

So, while everyone around me was growing and expanding and moving into the future with certainty and excitement, I was stuck in a cycle of nothingness. Day in and day out. I think it's why I am now obsessed with movement and every time I feel a lull I feel as though I've regressed completely. It still has a say in my current life. The threads still pull at me from a time long ago.

I limped through the remaining years of school with zero idea of what to do with myself, so I didn't do much. I worked jobs here and there to try to formulate some semblance of normality and meaning. One thing I had that was a constant was the guitar. It had gotten me through some seriously difficult periods because I could just sit and be taken away. Music touches my soul like nothing else. I had no idea that it would be my reintroduction to the land of the living years later when I ran into my old high school best friend at the casino one night.

He was a drummer, and in high school we fantasized about being in a famous band like *Metallica* and *Guns N' Roses* touring the world and creating art which inspired us. The problem was, I wasn't a good enough guitar player then. He had a few years of drums behind him already when we were 15, and I didn't start playing guitar until I was 15. For three years prior to that, I was a trumpet player. We'd both played in the school bands, but we knew we wanted to play heavy metal music.

I turned my attention from the trumpet to the guitar when I became completely obsessed with the instrument, mainly thanks to Slash from *Guns N' Roses*. It touched my soul so deeply (and still does) that I used to long to learn to be proficient enough to be able to recreate those beautiful sounds myself. But that takes time. And when we ran into each other years later, I was a much better player, and he was already in a band and they were looking for a guitar player. So, we caught up after about three years of losing contact, and he came and watched me play in my room. Then he said, "Do you want to come and have a jam?" I was so excited and nervous but was able to pick up what the guys were playing enough for them to ask me to be their guitar player. I was ecstatic. I had a really hard time interacting with new people and would never have thought to put myself out there as anything, let alone a guitar player. Having that mutual connection helped pave the way for my trajectory to alter significantly and break the cycle of nothingness.

We jammed a lot. I finally had something to put some focus into, and we just enjoyed hanging out. I was introduced to new friends and new experiences where people enjoyed my company and I enjoyed theirs. They didn't judge my appearance or want anything from me, which I wasn't used to. It took some adjusting for me, but it was a glimmer of hope. Of course, though, when alcohol was involved, things would start to surface, dark things I'd thought I'd shoved far enough into the shadows. I would also be so drained from using all of my energy in being around people that I would have to retreat into myself for days to recover. Even now, I get incredibly emotionally drained after even being on stage playing a gig, or being involved in interactions at all, that I need my alone time to reset myself. It's how I recharge.

So, while I had some good things happening in my life, I was still struggling and fighting the lack of growth I felt I was experiencing. Life is a multi-dimensional thing; there were many areas I wasn't taking care of, things that were really tearing apart the good foundations I was trying to establish. I've realised how necessary it is to manage and maintain all the dimensions of life to achieve equilibrium. One thing can take you and everything out entirely if it's not cared for. My friends could see this and would often experience this when I was with them and we were drinking heavily. And drinking the heaviest was usually me. I was self-destructive and self-loathing which would bubble up and start to show itself gradually through the veneer of the persona I had tried to keep up with when I was with others. I thought I could keep my dark parts hidden. But they could see I was struggling. And how do you deal with that? It's not easy.

These episodes were quite frequent and made myself and others uneasy. One, in particular, involved me taking a knife to my stomach and chest just to try and relieve the pain I was feeling. Then I walked the eight hours to my house in the middle of the night before passing out exhausted. My mate was incredibly confronted by the image of the open wounds and blood-stained clothing. As was I. Another one was spending my 23rd birthday in hospital getting stitched up for smashing a pint glass on my own head the night before and bleeding profusely all over the pub we were in, being told the wait in hospital would be a long one so heading back to a mate's place to drink and smoke speed with a makeshift bandage, which another drunken mate put together. Not things I wanted my family to see, that's for sure. And my mates often didn't see just how bad I was struggling, either. Just the surface level, or even the more humorous struggling if there is such a thing.

I also kept most of my struggles from my family, except I couldn't hide the fact that I was shutting myself off from them. I now know they worried constantly about me but didn't know what to do. Perhaps it's another reason why I couldn't tell them how bad I was or how bad I was getting. At one point I decided to take myself to get some help. One day I organized a psychiatrist's appointment hoping to be medicated or given something to sort out my mind. I turned up to the appointment still drunk, reeking of booze and having driven my friend's car to the appointment. We talked for 45 minutes and I hoped for something more than what I got. But I did get a script, so I was happy.

One of the things with antidepressants that is not recommended, like the aforementioned acne medication, is drinking alcohol. But that wasn't going to happen. I just did what I did with the acne meds and smashed my body with everything to see what would happen. Sure enough, they seemed to work a little. I wasn't quite reaching the depths of hell within myself that I was before. It was different, as I wasn't used to seeing the world like this. I had some hope instilled by the process. I'd started to actually think about a future. And not one where I wasn't around, although that still followed me for many years.

I was actually starting to see how I could make changes in my life and start to take myself where I wanted to head. That was a new and daunting concept. But also exciting. As music had provided such healing for me, I started to take more control of the band dealings and started to put energy and focus into music in general. Little did I know that I would, in a short period of time, meet the love of my life through the music scene.

There was a particular night at one of our gigs where my now-wife and I were actually supposed to meet, yet, luckily, we didn't, as I didn't exactly put on a good display. I proceeded to get incredibly drunk, got clipped by a car while running across the road, passed out in an alleyway in the city, and was picked up by the police. Not exactly an example of boyfriend material. So, when we did meet a month later, I was actually nursing a major hangover and was remaining sober for the night, which was lucky for both of us. She could also really see through my exterior to the depths of my soul and knew what was in there, good and bad, and didn't care. She was there unconditionally, without question. Have you ever met someone like that? It's incredibly special, and I am incredibly blessed.

I didn't realize she too had some major challenges and used alcohol as a way of coping and trying to get through life. We initially spent a lot of time talking online, as I was still painfully shy at times, locked away in a struggle with myself, or feeling unworthy of interactions. Because of this, I used the online platform to connect with her. The more we connected, the more we grew to like each other, and yet I still hadn't disclosed the totality of my struggles, which I was terrified of doing because I thought she would run as had so many before. So, when we were meant to meet for a date and I wasn't feeling good. I told her what that meant. She didn't run. She was there for me and, with loving curiosity, asked me about it. Our relationship grew deeper from there, in that moment, and we're now nearly at 10 years of marriage with unconditional love and connection, with every possible trial and tribulation you can imagine, but still standing strong with a beautiful little son in tow.

Not only did my wife give me something I didn't feel worthy of, but she also put me on a path which I didn't realize I needed but had always been searching for. Our honeymoon provided me with something that profoundly changed my life forever. It helped me put everything into perspective that had happened in my life up to that point and helped me form a vision for the future. And the timing of it was incredible, as shortly before our wedding I found out something which rocked me down to the deepest parts of my being. It also explained a lot about my issues with identity.

Identity has always been a struggle for me. Who am I and what am I here to do? I still don't have it totally figured out, but I certainly am on the path and refining it all the time. My various passions are being engaged, and I'm 35 years old, which is an interesting place to be due to not having any plans beyond 30, not thinking I would be blessed to have the opportunity, so now I'm improvising.

Turning 30 made me really look at what I actually wanted for myself going into the future and to be fulfilled: sitting within a loving marriage and sobriety for four years, the foundations for my life were stable enough to finally start putting down some structures. I floated around for so long with incredible sickness of the soul. I felt as though I had just wasted so much of my life, loathing my existence, drugs, booze, no direction, no purpose, no plans, no prospects or idea what I was doing here. This was all before I had the knowledge of something that would take my identity crisis to a crushing magnitude; the news that my father was actually my stepfather, and my biological father had left when I was a baby. I came across this news completely by accident, and I was 26 years old at the time.

How this came up was in conversation one night while we were at my parent's house for dinner and discussing the upcoming wedding and how I was five when my mum and dad got married. And Mum said something in regard to meeting my stepdad when I was two. The conversation continued, although I was stuck on that particular point trying to process what was just said. Then I mentioned that timeline and things got awkward. Mum said, "Do you remember before that?" I didn't but pretended I did, and the conversation continued on as we were all trying to make sense of what was happening. Most of all me, while I was in a head spin trying to deduce what was happening.

When we got into the car I said to my fiancée, "Did you hear what Mum said?" "No what about?" "I think she was telling me that my dad isn't my dad." "No way! You are both so alike," she said. I then calculated the maths for my fiancée, and some of what mum had said afterwards, and she thought for a moment as we pieced it together. Then it set in.

I cried for quite some time. Here I was at 26 years old trying to come to terms with this news, and so many questions followed. I spoke to my mum and stepdad and organized for them to come to my fiancée's house for dinner the next night to have a proper chat about it. That discussion helped me come to terms with things, and them, too. They had assumed I'd known the whole time, due to the fact that I was roughly two years old when they met, and I referred to my stepdad by his name for a long time. But there had never been good time to clarify my knowledge and my parents didn't want to add to the trouble, so it took until I was in a really good place for my mum to elaborate on the story in the discussion we had.

But it still floored me for quite some time. Until our honeymoon where my perspective widened quite significantly. I learnt an incredible amount from that experience. I don't harbour any resentment towards my parents and can see their perspective completely. And it helped clarify a lot about my struggle with identity and feeling somewhat of an outsider for the longest time.

Then during the aforementioned honeymoon, I accidentally fell onto a path I truly needed yet hadn't known existed. It was one I had no idea my wife had so desperately needed also about 12 years before, and it had saved her life.

We were about seven days into our beautiful two-week honeymoon together in Cairns, our favourite holiday destination. We adored Port Douglas, too, so we made the trip between the two every day, enjoying the sun and sights as a newly married couple. It was mid-afternoon, and we were wandering through the shopping precinct in Cairns when we stumbled across a really cool looking book shop called

Crystal Ball Bookstore. We wandered in. I had been having some neck troubles for a couple of days, and my wife suggested I have a Reiki treatment, as the signage said they did treatments there. I had no idea about the concept of Reiki, or even most of the books, crystals, and cards in the store. So, I proceeded to approach a staff member and ask for a Reiki session, and she motioned to someone else in the store and said, "Reiki?" And he said, "Okay," and took me into a treatment room.

He was a fairly short and slender man, perhaps in his 50s, with a ponytail. He had a strong accent, which I thought was French. He motioned for me to sit down and he sat across from me and pulled out a deck of tarot cards. As I said before, these concepts were foreign to me, but I was quite sure that Reiki wasn't sitting at the table with cards. But something in me wanted to see where this was going so I just let him continue the process. He shuffled and dealt the cards and got me to choose a cut. Then he proceeded to give me a rundown of my life. I couldn't believe the precision and accuracy. These weren't just generalized and abstract meanings and readings that were coming up; they were deep insights into my current and future trajectory. I had disclosed nothing and was read like a book. The time passed so quickly; I was in a daze. In that time, my wife had bought a couple of books and was waiting outside for me when eventually I floated out. I felt like I was literally floating on Cloud Nine.

"What happened in there?" my wife asked. I was wearing the biggest smile you could imagine and I was carrying myself differently and noticeably. "I just had a card reading and it was completely amazing!" I said excitedly. I told my wife about it and she was excited for me too. I asked her what she'd bought, and she showed me the books she had bought without me having any idea what this path had done for her. So, for the rest of the day we talked deeply about the spiritual path, the synchronicities, and circumstances that had led to us to meet in the first place and which put us in the exact time and place we were now and how.

We reflected until the mid-morning and then at some stage started to think about the future. We started to write out what we wanted. Future plans, mantras, rituals, and gratitude. For once in my life, I felt as though a compelling future was more in my control and that setting up some positive frameworks would help me govern myself in the present to pave the way for the future. Mental rehearsal and visualization excited me and became a part of my practice from then on. Before that I'd had no practices whatsoever. I'd just dealt with whatever came.

Once this became a part of deciphering the world, I was able to view my past and present experiences with greater clarity and understanding. Whenever I'm stuck, I still remind myself that things are as they are, exactly as they should be.

It was about four days after this life-changing interaction that I made a commitment to something I and many others didn't think was possible; I had my last drop of alcohol and said no more. We had been drinking on our honeymoon, and it was then I started to get the sense that I had a decent aversion or even allergy to it when I'd have one can of beer and feel off. Sure, everyone knew I had a lot of problems with alcohol, but that showed just how much. The funny thing is that because of my problems with alcohol there nearly wasn't a honeymoon or a wedding. I'd already made a mess of our engagement party and our hen's and buck's day, where I'd tried to throw myself out of a moving car doing 100k's an hour for the second time in a month, after having done the same at a friend's wedding.

My drunken antics were always a nerve-racking experience for those around me, as they never knew the unpredictable nature of what was in store. Neither did I. But it was after years of watching it happen that it finally came to a head and my then-fiancée sat around a table with our friends while I was passed out in bed. This was after the hen's and buck's night fiasco when they all expressed their concerns about us actually being married while I was like this. I had no idea that was happening until my wife said that she didn't care if I drank on our wedding day, but if she cried herself to sleep, then we were done.

This was a decision I needed to hear but which was ultimately up to me. It was a beautiful way of articulating her feelings and fears, but not in a controlling way. She knew it would sit deeply within me and I was in control. Sure enough, I was able to behave myself enough to get through the day, and we fell asleep together with smiles on our faces after such a beautiful day. So, two short weeks later I decided I was done. I'd never wanted to continue to live with alcohol being such a large part of our lives as it is for so many others, and I'd said for years that I want to move through life and have a family without drugs and booze. So, I grabbed the remaining bottles we had and cemented the intention by pouring the alcohol down the sink saying, "I'm done with this shit! No more!"

Funnily enough, I didn't even really have a plan or a way of doing it. But I knew it was done. My wife said, she would support me when we got home by not drinking also and then that was that. It's been nine years now, and sure there were some situations early on where I'd have a really strong desire to drink myself into oblivion, but nothing that some positive reinforcement and talking through couldn't help. My life was much better without it and I threw myself into many other things without always letting alcohol get in the way.

One of the big things was how do I remain in band playing gigs in pubs and do it? The truth is, I made adjustments. Changed my routines, cemented better habits, or prepared coping mechanisms. The journey of self-discovery, growth, expansion, and learning that was born out of this period of time was immense and still continues to this day and as far as I can see will always continue. Growth is the one word which I feel sums up my entire ethos. If I'm not growing, I'm miserable. In a sense, if we aren't growing then we are all dying. And to me it's meant constant and never-ending improvement. The smallest incremental and seemingly insignificant changes, which may not even appear to be happening, are always bubbling under the surface creating ripples of change. The adverse experiences have given me incredible insights and chances for growth, and so have the good experiences. It doesn't all have to be bad. I have to remind myself of this often.

So, having started married life back at home, post honeymoon and without drugs and alcohol, meant my mental health had started to improve. I was still medicated and still had my challenges, of course. In fact, maybe even more so because I wasn't masking them with drugs and alcohol. When a series of events left us completely broke—and broken in every sense of the word—it was hard not to want to drown it all out with substances. My band imploded, and I lost my friends and brothers. My wife's business partner left her to struggle unbelievably by pushing her out of the company she had helped to build. And for a long time, we struggled in every sense of the word. But we always had each other, and we knew that. We also would grow together. So, when we were struggling, we'd find a way to grow and do it together. Or one of us would read something, study something, or go to a workshop and give the other one the chance to catch up so we didn't leave each other behind. And, of course, along the way we were starting to think about our future and the subject of having kids.

We tried to do everything right and sought consultation with specialists to ensure we were creating every chance of success even if we weren't in the best position to do so. But things were slowly starting to mend while we were trying to conceive for quite some time. Then, one Valentine's Day weekend, we had a beautiful couple of days away in a resort where we played golf, ordered room service, hung out, and watched movies. After we checked out, on our way back home we stopped past our favourite town, Daylesford, for lunch and to spend some time in the spiritual shops. Little did we know we were about to have the most profound experience in quite some time and something which reminded us to be aware of our spiritual nature and path. And, funnily enough, one part involved my old mates the Tarot readers.

We were in a homewares store looking at candles when suddenly this woman approached my wife and said she had something for me and that something had pulled her into the store and told her that she had to give these beautiful Egyptian papyrus scrolls to me. This was mind-blowing and incredibly odd, as I'd never seen this woman in my life. "I am going into hospital and I may not make it out of there, so if I don't, I don't want anyone to just throw these out, as they are incredibly special to me and apparently you are the one who will take care of them," she said.

It was eerie, yet beautiful, and we were all a little unsure of what was happening here. "Ever since I was a kid, I've had a fascination with Egypt and have always felt a deep connection to everything involving Egypt," I said to her and observed these beautiful framed pictures. "I don't want anything for them," said the woman, and my wife insisted she have something for them and reached into her purse and pulled out some cash for her. We exchanged hugs and went our separate ways completely unable to process what that exchange was.

My wife and I sat down to lunch and decided it was time I had another tarot reading after that incredible experience, so we wandered down to book in. Luckily, the only reader had an opening right then (of course) so we sat in the room and he shuffled the deck and said a few things about me he had no prior knowledge of (of course) and he asked me what I'd like to focus on. One of the things I said was kids. He thought for a moment and said to both of us, "Don't worry about it. When you let go of trying, it will come. And actually I have a feeling you're going to be a dad in nine months." Then he corrected himself and said, "I mean, I have a feeling you'll be pregnant in nine months." Amazingly, this Freudian slip turned out to be exactly what the tarot reader said, because, sure enough, five days later we found out we were three weeks pregnant. This was another reminder to stay on the path, and it helped me clarify even further what I was working towards.

When our son came along, there was no way to describe the magnificence of that moment. As scary as it can be knowing you are responsible for another life, I felt ready. I knew I'd never be more ready, and it was time to put all the things into practice I'd worked on for years. There are little words in our language to describe the beauty of the experience of the birth of one's child. It was the most inspiring moment of my life and the cue to get my shit together even more so. Part of that was getting into the best shape of my life so that I could be as active as I needed to be for our little man, but also for myself, my current and future health, and maintenance of mental health.

I'd trained in the gym flat out and also trained in a few different martial arts (I was especially passionate about Muay Thai and still am) but for the longest time, injuries had stopped me from doing as much, and I didn't commit to training hard enough through it. I would regularly be out of action with body issues and I knew it would affect my activity with my son who, of course, was going to be active. I had no idea just how much. While participating in an online coaching program, one of my goals was to start this home workout program which was six days a week for three months to strengthen me from inside out. I committed to another three different programs after this first one and have continued training almost every day.

I learnt an incredible amount about myself on that first program, and I became obsessed with it from day one. I'd never committed to something of that magnitude before, and I saw what I was capable of, even when I was suffering internally with mental health issues, fatigue, lack of motivation, or severe time restrictions. Since that journey began three years ago, I have remained in the best condition of my life and am now able to commit myself to so much more activity than I ever have due to barely carrying any injuries, and if I have incurred any, I am able to continue despite injuries, rather than throwing it in altogether.

What does all of this mean? To me, it means that once I oriented myself towards growth, my life took off! It meant discovering meaning and purpose and progressing towards my best life. It hasn't been easy, but I continue to push myself in incremental ways every day. I have discovered that my entire life revolves around growth, and I am in my happy place when I'm immersing myself in knowledge and application.

After dealing with my own mental illness, addictions, challenges, and lack of meaning or purpose about the reason I'm even here, I've been blessed to be able to help those who also have challenges even greater than I could imagine, and now I teach them to do the same. And with each evolutionary unfolding in my own journey, I realize the things which make my soul dance and sing and ensure I engage in them in some small way. The end goal or outcome isn't even the concern for me. It's the joy of being involved in my passions, however varied they may be. But one thing that remains a constant for me is staying true to my path and growth.

"Believe in yourself
and all that you are.
Know that there is
something inside
you that is greater
than any obstacle."

~ Christian D. Larson

CHAPTER EIGHT

Shifting from Self-Pity to Self-Care

By Kate Williams

Have you ever wondered why some people, at their lowest, can fall victim to self-injurious behaviours in an attempt to numb their pain and cope with whatever they are going through, whilst others are able to rise above in a seemingly effortless fashion?

Rebuilding themselves, bettering their circumstances, and barely batting an eyelid as they smash through the roadblocks that would envelop others in an instant?

By definition, self-harm refers to any behaviour which involves the deliberate causing of pain or injury to oneself, usually as an extreme way of trying to cope with distressing or painful emotions. Cutting, burning or hitting yourself, binge-eating or starvation, or repeatedly putting yourself in dangerous situations are all forms of self-harm.

I want you to take a deep breath right now. Clear your mind of its daily chatter, and take a few moments to think about what your experience has been during your toughest challenges and lowest moments in your life to date.

Have you knowingly sabotaged yourself further at these times? Perhaps you've engaged in harmful behaviours willingly to avoid those unwanted feelings, or unwillingly, yet felt powerless to alter your actions? Or are you one who has already worked out how to forge ahead? Are you one who welcomes the opportunity for change or refinement with open arms? Or are you someone who has mastered their shield, and summons their strength with ease?

One of my mentors once said that our minds are like computers and our thoughts are like the software and programs installed – both of which we get to choose before the download commences. That analogy has always stuck with me. It. Just. Makes. Sense.

Just as it is recommended of your computer's health to undertake regular virus checks to keep it performing, I certainly agree the same should be true of our minds.

Think of what can happen if you allow a virus to sit within your computer for too long. It can spread incredibly fast, right? Your programs may start malfunctioning. Some of your data could be destroyed, and at worst your hard drive is completely corrupted.

I mean, it's pretty common these days that someone on the other side of the world can hack into your computer and hold you hostage to some extent, making you pay a ransom to reclaim your personal information, or other sensitive data within your hard drive!

It provokes some profound thoughts that similarly, if you allow negativity to fester within your mind for too long, your mental space will be held hostage, spiraling you deeper and darker into despair and making it harder to climb back out of.

In my experience, one of the largest factors in how long you stay at rock bottom always comes back to your ability to control what is 'planted' and grows within your mind, and the level of self-belief you have built in yourself to that day.

Before we go any further, I want you to know that whatever you are going through right now, whatever your struggles are, I believe you can come out the other side of them.

And as much as you probably don't want yet another person telling you that the challenges in front of you are necessary or warranted...they are. There isn't a single person on this planet who becomes a better version of themselves without challenges.

It is the challenges we face, after all, that spurs growth and along with pain, enforces action.

When our pressure points are heavily burdened, change is trying to inch its way in. It calls to us, waiting for us to acknowledge and harvest it.

Pain leads us to new beginnings. Pain teaches us about our strengths. It creates a new space within our lives for people who will treat us differently (better!), for those who will help us soar to new heights.

I've learnt over the years and now share with my clients that feeling pain can lead to magnificent things; that if you can learn to embrace it, channel it, and continue to look after yourself throughout the process of it, you will always have enough fuel to break through your current limitations and reach a new level in your life.

As an Adolescent, I had Such an Impressionable Mind

I was a naïve young girl, searching for answers as to who I was meant to be and where I fit in the world. I longed to feel like I mattered, like I was special. Constantly chasing these feelings left me focusing on my 'lack', and led me to partake in things my soul will forever scream at me for. I searched for intimacy in all the wrong places. I succumbed to peer pressure and dabbled in drugs. I abused my body and cheated on my morals over and over again. I just wasn't equipped with the knowledge of how else to fill my needs back then, and my vision was clouded by the pressures I felt to 'belong' and to be validated.

Even though I had fleeting moments where I felt like I was enough, for the most part I felt invisible regardless of what I did. It was a lonely journey indeed.

I compared myself to others and dreamt of having the same things I thought they had; beauty, direction, confidence, courage, love.

I built a name for myself as that friend who would help anyone in any way I could. I found importance in being a part of the solution to another's pain, and in a way, I guess it deflected from having to deal with my own for the most part.

It was always difficult though, when the tables turned and I realised there was no one really ever there to help me. This was when I felt my lowest. This is when I wished I was somebody else – anybody else, and would punish myself for not being 'worthy'.

The world around me appeared so superficial, and throughout those adolescent years, I grew to believe at the most basic level that having outward raw beauty and a thin stature equaled worthiness – over and above that of talent and intelligence.

Seeing as I felt I didn't have much of any of those characteristics, my level of self-worth never actually surpassed neutral or positive ground back then.

I fell victim to placing far too much emphasis in other people's opinions and the stories I had created around a number of less than desirable circumstances. As that was what I focused on, it, of course, was all I could see around me. As you can imagine, the evidence I collected around my lack of the above-mentioned traits was surmountable. I well and truly remained in the negative when it came to thinking of myself as having any sort of value for the majority of my adolescent years.

A Defining Moment

A defining moment that cemented my lack of worth in my mind was the first time my heart was severely shattered in my early twenties.

Have you ever suffered a broken heart? Did it feel to you like your whole world had stopped? I remember feeling like I couldn't breathe. I ached all over from the betrayal and pain. He was someone I would have turned my entire world upside down for...someone I thought I loved.

I remember the feeling as my body temperature rose instantly when another woman approached me at a bar and told me she had been sleeping with my boyfriend.

My cheeks, neck and ears shone a brilliant red as I wondered how many other people knew what had been going on. I felt incredibly stupid and wondered how I could have been so blind! I couldn't move as she shared her story with me of how he'd torn her friendships apart by sleeping around in her circle. The shame and embarrassment of having a promiscuous boyfriend slapped against me in waves as I sifted through the archives of my memory, ferociously searching for any missed clues that otherwise would have saved me that pain. It was all there, in plain sight now. One by one, her details all lined up, realisation stinging my ears. Funnily enough, she'd recognised me from a photobook I'd made him; otherwise I might never have known.

How many of my so-called 'friends' had pretended in my presence, yet were in on the secret, covering for him? This woman was the only one brave enough to come forward, and for that I was actually very grateful, albeit pained.

I felt like I had no one I could trust and that the whole world was laughing at me; laughing at me for believing, even for a second, that I was worthy of a happy ending.

Following that event my self-talk was brutal! It had to be me, right? I wasn't pretty enough. I wasn't skinny enough. I wasn't fun enough. The woman from the bar was younger and more attractive than I was. I picked on everything I thought was wrong with me. Surely I had done something to him to make him treat me this way? I told myself I was so foolish to believe anyone would ever love me completely, what, with all my flaws and all.

I locked out the world and became a shell of myself for almost six months.

I still managed to go to work, somewhat robotically, but my thoughts were dark and kept me caged in my grief. I'd barely make eye contact with customers or my colleagues. Conversations were short and I was quick to put my hand up for any solo tasks so I didn't have to be around too many people.

After work I would rush straight home and retreat to the safety of my bedroom. I avoided my flatmate as much as possible. Part of me wanted someone to notice my pain…anyone to care enough to check up on me, to hold me and tell me everything would be okay; yet I told myself that I wasn't worthy of that – that no one cared. In hindsight, I actually made it nearly impossible for anyone to be close to me during those months.

I tried to shut out my thoughts by blasting music in my ears. I attempted to drown my sorrows in bottle after bottle, but ended up hating on myself even more when I was drunk. I sobbed alone, and often.

I was so repulsed by myself that I didn't want to eat, believing that starving myself was the only way anyone was ever going to love me.

The problem was, I barely made it two days without food. I remember hating myself even more for not being able to starve myself properly, and thinking I was a pathetic waste of space.

Changing myself consumed every thought, so I came up with a 'Plan B' instead. 'This is what will make you skinnier. Worthier. Prettier', I thought to myself. I'd abstain from food for as long as I possibly could and then allow myself to binge on whatever I wanted, usually in front of my flatmate so I wouldn't arouse any suspicion. After ravenously devouring the contents of my plate, I'd excuse myself quickly to the bathroom or nearest toilet where I'd run the shower or tap to hide the fact I was sticking my fingers down my throat and purging, before too many calories could be absorbed into my body.

My mental state was such that the look on my face when I had hundreds of burst blood cells around my eyes and upper cheeks somehow made me feel less empty. They were the result of my body gasping for air while it obeyed my repeated command, carrying out my punishment. It made me feel like I was finally doing something for myself. Something to change the person I no longer wanted to be.

I didn't stop there. I worked myself to the point of exhaustion through exercise, all the while focusing on what my life would be like when I was skinnier. I'd rant to myself that what I was doing wasn't good enough, and I had to go harder. Occasionally I'd get pins and needles pricking and pinching throughout my limbs. I would become light-headed, spots forming in my vision and the sound of my weakened heart thumping loudly in my ears. Only then would I allow myself to stop. I could never let my guard down and praise myself or say I'd done a good job. There was no enjoyment. It was like I was possessed. I hated my reflection in the mirror, and would look at myself in disgust, silently screaming things to myself you'd never dare say to anyone out loud.

Every time I ate, I would tell myself that I was a failure, a waste of space. I would get so angry at myself for needing to eat. I wasn't in control of anything! I was never going to be 'one of those girls' that was naturally beautiful. No one thought I was pretty, and no one ever would. I had nothing to offer the world. I was worthless. I began thinking about how no one would even care if I was here anymore, and maybe I was better off dead. So much negativity festered in my mind and kept me in the darkest place I'd been up until that point in my life.

Looking Back

Looking back, I'm not even sure how I got out of that place, how I managed to eventually move on. Perhaps it was a song, a book, or a person who helped me snap back to reality...I honestly couldn't tell you. I guess the pain eventually got less and I began to build some of the control back over my thoughts and emotions over time.

The behaviour, however, had become engrained in my subconscious. For years, whenever I was faced with high anxiety-inducing events or circumstances, particularly when my self-worth was being threatened or I felt like I was being personally attacked in some way, it wouldn't take much for these thought patterns and behaviours to resurface as my coping mechanism.

Around three years ago, in my early thirties, I was sitting in an armchair at a session with a life coach, when a profound realisation hit me like a tonne of bricks.

Nothing in my life would flourish until I first allowed myself to flourish. Nothing could be okay, great, or phenomenal even - in any area of my life – until I was first those things within myself.

I'd gone to see the life coach on a friend's recommendation because I'd had enough of waking up every morning thinking that this wasn't the life I'd signed up for, and I wanted 'out'. I was sick of focusing on all the things I didn't have, and then feeling incredibly guilty for ignoring those things I already had.

I was desperate for change because going around and around in circles was sucking the life right out of me. Metaphorically drowning and stuck in a cranky, miserable and incredibly low mood for the umpteenth time had my thoughts becoming darker with every passing day.

My businesses weren't where I felt they should be, my marriage was at a crossroads, my family felt like it was being torn apart, I was being personally attacked by family and acquaintances, and to top it all off, my relationship with food had become the polar opposite of my younger days and I was emotionally eating everything in sight. I was all over the place and couldn't see any opportunities to change my position.

Rock bottom can look like a thousand different things to each and every one of us, and unfortunately isn't something we have the option of only hitting once in our lives.

Guidance

This time round, luckily for me, I had some guidance.

I changed the questions I was asking myself and learned to be more resourceful as a result. When previously feeling like everything was worthless, I'd blamed it all on myself. I'd dwell on the 'why me' thoughts. The 'what did I do to deserve this' and the 'when am I ever going to catch a break' questions swirling around in my mind could never, ever motivate me because the answers to all of those questions were blaming, shaming and hating on myself, none of which is ever very productive or life-enhancing!

By simply changing the 'What', 'Why' and 'When' to 'How', I allowed my mind to find alternate ways of approaching the many challenges I was facing. Try it! Next time you're feeling like quitting something, ask yourself 'How would I go about this if I knew I couldn't fail'?

Believe me when I say that the variations of this question are the hugest pain in the ass and frustration when you're not used to using them! Your mind may shout a defiant "I don't know!" over and over, but little by little, the more you allow yourself to sit quietly and ponder, I promise things you'd never considered before will start popping into your mind as the resource centre within your brain expands.

I'm not telling you it is easy to do this. But just like everything else, practice will get you closer to mastery than ignorance ever will, and I believe our power lies in a handful of simple shifts to catch ourselves before falling too deep into a downward spiral.

Asking yourself better questions is a powerful way to rebuild your foundations and strip back all of the bullshit you've adopted over the years from previous thought patterns, belief systems, behaviours, and other people that no longer serve you. I'm an avid list maker, so for me, really going deep into the layers of how I've come to feel a certain way or build a particular belief is always the first step.

Secondly, I focus on shifting my belief toward where I want it. I look for examples of where I or someone else has done what I'm saying I can't, or pushed through where I'm stuck. So many skills and events are transferrable, and if we collect enough evidence from these examples it becomes easier to find the motivation and direction required to push forward.

You must consciously make an effort to nurture both your mind and body. It's astounding how irritable, frustrated and closed off you can be when you're not taking focused care of yourself. Sleep patterns, nutrition and exercise for your body, and meditating in a way that feels natural to you for your mental health and to keep out those unwanted thoughts is vital when surging through obstacles.

Meditating is massively misunderstood if you ask me, and doesn't have to be the 'sit down cross legged with your pointer finger and thumb touching humming Ommmmm' kind, either. It can be as simple as taking time out for yourself by doing an activity that connects you to your happy place, allowing your mind a moment to be free from your worries. Drawing, stretching, journaling, writing out gratitudes, colouring in and visualising your goals are all fantastic ways to lose yourself in a space made for releasing pent up stress.

If you don't have something like this in your life right now, I recommend you start experimenting and find one.

Look for a support person or group. Grab an exercise buddy and get out in nature to move your body. Learn new sports. Take new classes. Go play on the playground equipment at your local park, with or without your kids. Better yet, go and do it alone, with your partner, or best friend and let that carefree child come out! It is important to find something that can create a space to help realign you.

One of the biggest lessons we can learn is to practice being kinder to ourselves. It has taken me a long time to realise that no matter what life throws at us, we absolutely can find the strength to overcome what is in front of us. Such strength however, doesn't just magically appear and at times we have to reach deeper for it than we feel able.

Recognise that talking down to yourself for not being good at something is bullying! Treating yourself like shit because you can't do it all on the first attempt will cause you to quit before you've ever really begun. Make the decision to never say anything to yourself that you wouldn't say to your child, partner or anyone else that you love.

Don't ever allow yourself to stop dreaming. Some our greatest ideas come to us through our dreams, pushing us to research, plan and practice new approaches that could be exactly the missing link we're needing. Allow yourself to dream as big as your creativity and imagination will take you, but never forget to focus and celebrate each small win along the way to build your belief, courage and confidence.

When things don't appear to be working out the way you'd imagined, realise it is not failure or a reason to quit. It is an opportunity to go back to the drawing board and reinvigorate your actions from a more experienced angle. Never, ever, ever give up on your dreams.

It's certainly took me a while to grasp that we really do have a choice in how we react to challenging situations. We can choose to learn and grow from them, or be swallowed whole and consumed every waking second by them, just as my younger self did before I knew any better.

You see, my younger self was so caught up in being validated that she couldn't possibly comprehend that the whole world wasn't going to like her, or 'get' her, and that that really was okay. In my wisdom, I can now see that there's not one person in the history of mankind that has never experienced 'haters'. She had to feel her own pain and witness her own behaviours and thoughts to be able to see how most people who throw out judgment and hurt towards others are in fact, just people who are hurting themselves, bringing others down to their level so they weren't so alone and distracting themselves from their own pain.

No one told her that there will always be a specific tribe out there for each of us; that if we live into our values and do as many of the things that bring us joy as we can, we will eventually attract these quality people into our lives, and our souls will dance with an abundance of happiness and deeper connection.

She'd never understood how important it is to listen to our emotions for clues; that if something felt 'off' and we were tuned in appropriately, we could adjust the frequency of our emotional state and bring necessary change into our lives almost instantaneously. It is only through facing her own difficulties that she could build that self-awareness.

You know that feeling when people are commenting on how amazing you look, whether it's because you've been working out or you're wearing an amazing new outfit, or you've just accomplished something that makes you so proud that you glow from head to toe?

That feeling as a parent when your kids are happy, your partner is happy, and everyone is just in perfect harmony?

The rush of endorphins you feel when you engage in physical activity that you enjoy, whether it be team sports, gym training or even being intimate with your partner?

How does everything else in your life feel at that moment?

Does it drown out all negative thoughts? I may be imagining it, but I'm certain that even when facing extreme challenges, their emotional intensity or weight is significantly reduced because your brain has switched focus after receiving feel-good hormones in some way shape or form from an outside source, even if only for a few minutes.

Our minds simply cannot be dark and light, good and bad, happy and sad at the same time.

Will you join me in making some decisions right now? To be our own source. To look after our sleep and body rejuvenation. To be mindful about the foods we put into our mouths and how our bodies feel afterwards – what spikes less patience and more irritability – and reduce the culprits from our grocery baskets? To move our bodies intentionally, in some way that will bring a smile to our face and release thousands of milligrams of endorphins into our brains?

What if we included a decision to consciously speak kinder to ourselves? What if we'd practice on expanding our spirituality by meditating, scripting, keeping a gratitude journal, learning more about how balance and harmony in mind and spirit can make a monumental shift in the actions we take and what we focus on within our daily routines?

It's no secret that when you're feeling good from the inside-out, trivial, every-day nonsense has less chance of derailing you and adding to the weight of any current challenges you're facing. Think of a time when you felt absolutely amazing. Did you not feel as if you could take on the world?!

On a deeper level I feel we all know this, yet it's been made obvious to me throughout my own life, and to those that I have had the pleasure of coaching; far too often we allow ourselves to get trapped by unfortunate circumstances and make matters worse, or prevent ourselves from getting over, past, or through them when we stop caring about ourselves.

Don't you agree?

It is so important to look after our physical, mental and spiritual selves to be at our best, in the good times, but even more so in the hard times.

I honestly get goose bumps thinking about just how much my life has changed since beginning to practice these 'shifts'. Whilst it certainly hasn't happened overnight, they truly have allowed me to break away from the stale and dysfunctional relationship I had with myself and enjoy a life full of abundance.

If you too begin to implement these steps and allow yourself time to master some discipline, you will be able to shift the barriers and limitations you have imposed on yourself. Remember, if you get lost along the way, surround yourself with people who you can learn from and who will keep you accountable to your new standards. Practice building belief in your abilities in all areas of your life, and I guarantee your self-worth will skyrocket.

Go on. Try it. Let me know how much your life improves!

"Adversity and suffering
are two of life's greatest
teachers. Through them,
we learn how we can grow."

~ Unknown

CHAPTER NINE

Hidden Shinning Jewel

By Putu Cita

Bali is just a tiny island in the large archipelago of Indonesia that has a delightful charm and a special place in the heart of world travellers. The first known European contact with Bali is thought to have been made in 1512 by a Portuguese expedition followed by the Dutch explorers and later on followed by some other travellers. Many famous people come to Bali to witness the beauty of this tiny island and have even made Bali their home bases. A famous Spanish painter, Antonio Blanco, came to Bali for the first time in 1952, fell in love with his painting model named Ni Ronji. They got married in 1953 and made Ubud their home where they built a family together. Other famous people have come and visited Bali, too, from top Hollywood celebrities like Mick Jagger, Barbra Streisand, Julia Roberts to top successful business people like Sir Richard Branson, and top politicians such as the President of the United States of America, Barack Obama.

My name is Ni Luh Putu Cita Wati. Yes, it's quite a long name; therefore, I introduce myself as Putu Cita. Bali has been my home since I was born in 1982. Both of my parents are originally from Bali and both come from a background of farmers. My dad's family are from Denpasar, which is the capital city of Bali, whereas my mom's family come from a little village located west of Ubud called Abiansemal, which is still part of Badung regency.

In Bali, as part of the Indonesian government system, we follow the national law. And at the society level we have customary law that can't be separated between religion and custom. We can't define between religion and custom because all aspects of life are totally influenced by our Hindu religion. According to anthropologic science, there are three systems of families: patrilineal, matrilineal, and parental. These systems are exercised in different communities, and Bali practices the patrilineal system which is followed by the Hindu religion. What does this mean exactly? It means that only the man may become the leader of the family and the descendants must follow the line of the father. That is why, in Balinese culture, when a girl marries, the girl will then follow the boy and stay with her husband's family. However, when a family has only girls and no son, then the parents of the girl will give a note to one of the girls stating that when she finds a boyfriend, the boy must agree to move in and stay with the girl's family. Every new married couple will conduct their duty and obligation to their husband's society or with the wife, if the family has no boy descendant. With this patrilineal system in Balinese culture, we hope to have generations taking care of community responsibilities and preserving our culture.

I was born and grew up in Denpasar with my dad's family, where he had a total of 13 siblings. Six passed away when they were still babies (amongst them there were twins). The remaining seven siblings are my three uncles and four aunties, and my dad is child number six out of eight children who are still alive. In the old time, it was so common to hear that one Balinese couple has more than two children, and Balinese people have their own unique system of knowing their first child up to child number four, by adding a first name. There is Putu/Wayan, which means child number one; Made/Kadek is the second born; Komang/Nyoman is child number three; Ketut is the fourth born. And if a couple has more than four children, then the same name will apply back again to the child number five and so on. Therefore, when coming to Bali, people will get to know so many Putu or Made or Komang or Ketut because that is the identity of the Balinese people. And, yes, I am the first child, and I have two younger brothers and one younger sister.

Until the late 1990s, Dad was the first and only son who got married and had children, and I became the first grandchild in the family, based on the patrilineal system. Since I was born, I've gotten to know only my grandma from Dad's side of the family, whereas I spent most of the later stage my childhood with her. Dad told me that he was fortunate with his life, having graduated from high school, and after several job experiences with local businessman, he finally got a high-paying job at one of the state-owned enterprises called PLN (State Owned Electricity Enterprise). His job at PLN paid a high salary, and our family was able to afford luxury household items.

I remember in the late 80s, we already had a washing machine, fridge, DVD player, high quality stereo system, and a colour TV. And can you imagine, of course, my siblings and I were also provided with luxurious toys, too. Sometimes, as part of his job, Dad was sent for a few days to other islands around Indonesia, and during this time Mom would take care of me and my three siblings by herself, but on occasion she received help from our remaining family members who stayed with us in the same family compound. It is common practice in Bali that one family compound will have grandparents, aunties, uncles, parents, and the children all living together.

And I spent my childhood exactly in this family portrait. Being married to a Balinese family, the woman is not only responsible to take care of her husband and children but also to take care of all immediate family members who stay in the compound. For a few years, my mom took care of her husband with four children, my grandma, and four of Dad's siblings (three brothers and one sister). My mom was not just a housewife and a mother, but she also worked as a government employee, working in administration at one of the high schools in Denpasar.

My mom is my role model. She is such a loveable and super-caring person. From the age of eight, when I was on school holidays, I would often join Mom at her workplace. And to keep me quiet and patient while I waited for her, Mom would take me to the back desk where there was a vacant typewriting machine. Without hesitation, Mom showed me how the machine worked, provided me with blank paper, and left me playing alone.

Tik...tik...tik...tik...kliiiiinng...tik...tiik...tiik...kliiiing... Soon I found myself enjoying the process, and I mastered typing from a young age. When I was 15 years old, I already acted as secretary in my family when my late uncle bought a type writing machine that we later used to make contract letters.

As a girl with high curiosity, a spirit for learning was embedded in me since I was young. When other girls chose to spend their Sunday mornings having a long sleep, instead I would go to Mom, begging her to take me with her to the traditional market near our home. I would follow Mom everywhere from shop to shop, from one seller to the next one, while carrying the shopping bag for her. As my reward, Mom would feed me a special breakfast by getting our favorite dish of yellow rice or buy delicious Balinese porridge.

Over time, I realized that Mom not only gave me special delicious breakfast every Sunday, but I got to know how to bargain, a skill that I naturally learned from my mom and it really has helped me with my daily life when it comes to negotiation. Now, when I go to the traditional market and start to bargain with a seller, I have to giggle inside my heart because I see my mom in myself. Mom has been so caring with all of our family members, including to my married aunty, my dad's sister and her sister-in-law. Every time we had a Balinese festival celebration, Mom would be busy with cooking and baking for our family and also would share with her sister-in-law. We all would gather at home chattering and laughing out of love.

Family. What does it mean for you? What does it mean for me? Certainly, family has its own meaning for each of us. "Family is not an important thing. It's everything," said Michael J. Fox. That's what family means to me. I lived with my parents and my dad's siblings, a total of 10 of us living in one compound with three separate buildings. Our house is a very simple house with one building containing a kitchen where we used to gather in the afternoon and chatter whilst we enjoyed our early dinner.

Before the invention of the gas cooking method, most Balinese families would use fire wood as the method of cooking, and this is what I used, too. I can say that I was lucky to have watched this method of cooking when I was small. Our kitchen was totally black from the smoke of the fire wood that we used for cooking. Every time we wanted to cook, we put a few small, thin pieces of wood in the fireplace and made a flame out of it by blowing air from a bamboo pipe. If we didn't know how to do it properly, we would come out of the kitchen with a black face. And this happened to me one day when I wanted to boil water. After I had made the fire, I came out of the kitchen, and some family members were laughing at me. I did not know why they were laughing whilst looking at me until one aunty told me to find a mirror and see myself. Hahahaha…. I came out with make up like a clown with a shiny black nose, and soon we were all laughing. I found out that happiness is not about owning many things but about experiencing joy, pride, satisfaction, being grateful, and living life to the fullest. Happiness can exist in simplicity, and it can be one of the best moments or experiences in our lives.

As kids, our minds are usually only filled with words of play. Sometimes we forget to do our homework and—worst—we even forget to eat because we enjoy playing with friends or siblings. I had a great time playing with my siblings only until I was 10 years old. I have never imagined that I would grow up without my family, but that was the reality of my life. My dad got promoted at his work and had to move to Lombok, the island east of Bali, for an uncertain period of time. Very likely he would need to stay there until his retirement age. Mom, who had a job here in Bali, wasn't feeling good about leaving my dad alone in Lombok, so she arranged the paperwork to transfer her job to Lombok. Luckily, she got the same job and position at one of the high schools in Mataram, which is the capital city of Lombok.

The whole family was ready to have a new chapter of life in Lombok, except for myself who had to stay in Bali. I hardly remember how I felt and dealt with that situation the day when I was separated from my parents and my three other siblings. The only thing that I remember was, my parents told me the reason they could not take me with them was because I was the first grandchild in the family and that I was responsible to do the ceremony at home.

Amazingly, I must have had a big heart to accept that life can be tough, because I cannot remember whether or not I made a big protest for this unfair life circumstance that I faced at a young age. I had no choice, so I continued my life in Bali with my grandma, three uncles, and one aunty. Since that time, I was no longer sleeping with my siblings but with my grandma and aunty. Then, when my aunty got married and moved out following her husband, I slept together with Grandma. Two of my uncles were single all their lives, and one uncle finally got married, so he and his wife also lived in the same compound.

At that time, I already felt that life was hard on me, leaving me alone to grow up without my parents whom I needed in my teenage years. At one point, I felt that I was not being loved enough by my parents, and I started to resent them for leaving me in Bali. These feelings of sadness, disappointment, hatred, and not being loved were residing deep down inside me, causing an emotional separation with my parents. I felt like I was at rock bottom with no other options available to me at the time. I had no choice other than to accept my situation and continue my life with Grandma and Uncle, and that forced me to become an independent person at a young age.

Slowly, I started to take responsibilities like taking care of Grandma, maintaining the cleanliness of the house, doing the washing, helping with the cooking in the morning, and doing the daily ceremony. Well, not to mentioned that I was also responsible for myself. I can say that I have built a good level of awareness about life since I was very young. Imagine a young girl growing up with only her grandma and uncle, whilst she needed guidance and information about how to handle life, but that support wasn't available. So, in the journey of life, I became a mature person just from finding my own life path. The old saying, "you learn by doing it," is a perfect picture of how I learned to do many things in life.

For many girls, the teenage years are the best times of their lives, where they allow themselves to explore life freely in whatever way they want, mostly all at the expense of their parents. And this image was simply far from the way I had to grow up as a teenager. As young Balinese girls, we have many occasions for which we dress up with our beautiful traditional outfits to attend various religious and cultural celebrations. For my teenage years, I bought a flashy traditional outfit for myself only twice, and that was luxury for me. Most of the time, I would wear my grandma's outfit, or sometimes I borrowed one from another relative.

I remember one day when I had to represent my family at a social event in the community, and I received a brightly colored outfit from my relative who had much brighter skin than myself. I did not have much choice, and when I was ready to go, my uncle (child number seven) who was going with me, made a ridiculous comment about the outfit, and I was left with the feeling that I wasn't pretty because my skin color did not match the flashy-colored outfit that I wore. And over time, somehow, this feeling settled deeper into my heart, leaving me with no self-confidence. I felt that I had reached a low point in my life.

For some years, I lived with very low self-esteem to a point that I said to myself, "I have to do something extraordinary, something that will become my identity, something that will make me walk with pride." So, from that moment, I always said positive affirmations, acknowledging that I am a strong girl with a beautiful heart. And I gained strong self-confidence by being great at school and an excellent friend to others.

One of the best moments that makes me so proud of myself was when I was accepted into the second-best junior high school in Denpasar. In elementary school, I was always competing with two other female classmates as the top three best students in the class, and most of the time I would achieve second position. I am also quite proud that I am the only one in my family who can speak English fluently and the only one who has active conversations in English. Also, in the area of friendship, I am always friendly, cheerful, attentive, and concerned for other people. Because I have this disposition, people like to be friends with me.

As for the caring part, it must have developed due to my life experiences with Grandma and my uncle. They were such loving people, and I have an unusually strong relationship with them. One day, when I had a school holiday, my parents took me to Lombok so that I could spend some days with them and my siblings. Surprisingly for my parents, specially my mom, on the second day after I arrived in Lombok, I was crying out of sadness because I missed my grandma. I insisted that my parents bring me back to Bali so that I could be with Grandma again. I can imagine how confused my parents must have been seeing how attached I was to my grandma. And since that day, I never again spent my school holidays in Lombok with my siblings until I was 15 years old.

Both Grandma and my uncle took care of me very well. Occasionally I was spoiled with many good gifts and experiences, mostly created by my uncle, but most of the time I was a young girl with many responsibilities. The three of us would be busy early in the morning cooking in the kitchen, and every day I would get different tasks from my uncle which makes me the youngest master chef in the family. And this is how I came to like cooking, simply because of my earlier life experiences.

Life with Grandma and my uncle was quite colorful and full of deep emotion. Grandma is a warm-hearted, nurturing, active, disciplined, and responsible Balinese woman. And in some areas, she sets quite a high standard of living. I remember one day when I came to Grandma with the intention of wanting to help her with the weaving of dried banana leaves. It was my first try and it came out of shape and it didn't meet her standard, and she politely said to me that I'd better continue with my school homework.

I did not give up easily and I asked her why my weaving wasn't acceptable, especially since the weaving she made wasn't for us but to sell at the market? And Grandma said to me, "Whatever we make, whether it is for us or for other people, we should give the same quality of care and love." That answer was simply a bit heavy for me to digest at that young age. The wisdom did not stay with me at the time, so I continued taking the banana leaves and kept practicing my weaving until finally Grandma accepted my creations, and that made me happy. As Balinese people, we do a lot of weaving with palm leaves and dried banana leaves, which makes some of us Balinese people very creative.

My childhood was filled with so much wisdom for life that came from Grandma and Uncle. As a leader, Uncle had a lot of responsibility in our family, in our extended family, and in the community. Uncle had a very important role in my life, much more than my dad. Uncle is child number three of the eight children. He has never been married, and he left school early due to lack of money in the family. However, until the end of his life, Uncle was the most hard-working child in the family, and that helped to keep us alive until the time when Dad received his well-paying job. Both Uncle and Dad became the heroes of our family.

Uncle sacrificed his life by not taking a formal education at school and, instead, gave the chance to his younger brother and sister. When other kids were wearing their school uniforms, Uncle would be working with Grandpa wherever the job was and whatever the job was.

From what I have been told by Uncle and my dad, Grandpa was a super-diligent and disciplined person, but he also had a bad temper. No one in the family was brave enough to confront Grandpa and, in his life, there was no time for playing even for the kids. There was only work, work, and work. The outcome of being a very diligent person, Grandpa had been liked by many of the rich families in our hometown, and it became the gold entrance for my uncle. Through the contact and network of Grandpa, Uncle got to know one of the wealthiest families in my hometown of Denpasar, which became the starting point of his success.

In his life, Uncle has been recognized as the most successful man, not just in the family, but also in my hometown, and we all are so very proud of him. Coming from the background of a farming family with no formal education, Uncle finished his career as the head of pastry at one of the biggest hotel chains in Bali. At home, Uncle taught me and my siblings the basic rules of working in the kitchen by demonstrating how to hold a knife, how to cut vegetables quickly, and how to cook certain foods. What we all enjoyed so much was when we made our own fresh bread. On a national level, Uncle also had the chance to participate in an international pastry competition in Jakarta, where he competed with other chefs from around Indonesia.

Uncle was an avid storyteller, often sharing stories with us that included much life wisdom. On one fine day, Uncle took me, my two younger brothers, and another two boys from our extended family to the hotel where he worked. We went through the kitchen, and Uncle explained to us everything which we saw, gave us the longest bread we'd ever seen, and ended the tour by taking us to the top floor where we saw the wide-open ocean from the rooftop.

He taught me and the whole family that having a high degree at school is not a guarantee of a successful life, but that being diligent and having a good attitude is the key. Uncle is the best life coach I ever had. His wisdom taught me from the age of eight, which was difficult for me to understand at that time, but it has been stored well in my memory until now. And, only when I was well aware of the realities of life, I noticed the meaning of it and came to deeply appreciate his mission for teaching me all of his wisdom for living.

Although Uncle had never been married, his love and affection for me, my siblings, and the kids in our big family were pure. On the weekends, Uncle would often take us five kids to the Play Station House near our home and let us have fun with all kinds of games. And if we all behaved well during the week, each of us would get an ice cream after the playing time was finished. On such an occasion, Uncle would then give us another bit of life wisdom: whatever we do we have to have a plan. Then we would hear his quote: "Plan your work and work your plan."

Of course, we were all so young that Uncle must have felt that the quote didn't sink deeply into us. Therefore, he repeated it frequently, taking us often to the Play Station House and spoiling us kids there almost every weekend. And what was the result? The quote successfully sunk into all five of us, and whenever we have a family event or gathering, we would then be reminded by the quote and say to each other, "Plan your work and work your plan," followed by a happy smile for each other. Much of the fun that I experienced in my childhood was created by Uncle. He would do anything to give the best life to all his nephews and nieces and to our whole family.

My childhood was filled with lots of fun, and then it was suddenly taken away from me when I was 10 years old when I started to live in Bali with Grandma and Uncle. From the age of 10 until I was 16 years old, I had experienced a real-life journey where I dealt with all sorts of emotions by myself, and I took full responsibility for my life. Through this period of time, I learned the hardworking life, the life of being a farmer, where I worked in the field under the hot sun and forgot about having bright and smooth skin.

When I came to the rice field for the first time, I would do nothing other than to accompany my Grandma and Uncle. As soon as we arrived, I jumped to the small hut in the middle of the rice field, which was made by just four branches of trees, and I would play with a can which created noise and made the birds fly away from our paddies. And sometimes if Grandma and Uncle spent a longer time working, when they came back, they would find me asleep and snoring in the hut. It's so easy to fall asleep in the hut in the middle of the green rice field with a fresh breeze.

After taking me to the field several times, Uncle slowly changed the policy for me. He started giving me small tasks and letting me have the experience of working in the rice field. Until one day when Uncle must have decided not to continue planting rice anymore, we converted the land from the rice field into dry soil where we planted various vegetables and fruit trees, which we harvested regularly and received better income from the land.

We planted some 50 mango trees, 10 papaya trees, and we planted some hundred square meters of field with various kinds of vegetables such as spinach, long bean, eggplant, tomato, chili, and many of kinds of vegetables. Working in this natural field got me used to seeing and interacting with all sorts of animals, including snakes, rats, millipedes, leeches, and cockroaches. With this new project, I spent every afternoon in the field with Grandma and Uncle.

After having a short break once I came home from school, Uncle would take Grandma and me to the rice field where we would work. We would clean the field from the weeds and water all the plants, going around with buckets of water that we drew from the well by a rope. I was so fit at this time from the work in the field, and I definitely didn't need to go to the gym to build my muscles. But going to the field every day and working there did not always make me happy, especially when I saw other girls enjoying their time in different ways that looked like more fun than I was having.

I started to question myself. Why do I have to go through this hard life? Why did my parents leave me alone in Bali with Grandma and Uncle? Don't they love me? Why did this happen to me? I kept asking these questions to myself over and over. Sometimes I found myself crying in bed in the evening when I could not find the answers to these questions. I didn't have the courage to ask these questions to anyone in my family, and I decided to keep them to myself. When I asked these disempowering questions, my mindset was at rock bottom and everything felt like a hopeless mess.

At that time, I was already practicing mini mind shifts, in which I trained my mind not to feel pity about my life. And it worked quite well, leaving me with acceptance that I had no choice other than to join Grandma and Uncle in the field every day, and I started to build the hope that I would see the result of my work.

Amazingly, this thought automatically changed my mood, and I started to enjoy it a bit more. I became happy when seeing the fruit beginning to ripen on the trees. It was time for harvest. The three of us, Grandma, Uncle and myself, were busy picking up the mangos and papayas. We had so much fruit that we could sell, and Uncle already assigned me with a new task. Uncle prepared all the equipment that I needed to sell the mangos around to the small stall called *warung*. Except, he forgot to equip me with sales skills. So, naturally, I performed my new job as a sales person and became very excited as I got the piece of paper from the buyer—the paper that has value on it called money. At the end of the trip from selling the fruit, I gave all of the income to Uncle.

There was no agreement with Uncle about how much bonus I would get from selling the fruit, and it was never an issue for me. How surprising that Uncle gave me half of the income from selling the fruit. At that time, I received Rp 40.000. Uncle said to me that I could use the money to buy anything I wanted. I was jumping, full of excitement from earning my first pay, and I have loved working since then.

Uncle may have sensed this new spirit in me, and one day he came to me and shared another piece of wisdom for life. He said, "We are from a simple farm family, and we can only have what we want to have if we are working. If you want to change your life, you have to change it; nobody can help change your life. And one day, when you are grown up, remember to have your palm above and not on the bottom." For some years, I didn't know what Uncle meant with the last sentence, until one day he explained that he wanted me to be successful so that I can place my palm facing down (gesture of sharing what I have with other people who are in need), not being the one who asked for help (palm facing up).

After I have seen and received the results of working in the field and being successful as a street sales person, I learned much about loving myself and appreciating life. Having practiced the mind shift, I feel I am newly born with a different attitude towards life. I saved the money I received from selling the fruit until one day, with a feeling of pride, I went to the shoe shop and bought myself a pair of school shoes from my own income. I became a sales person when I was 13 years old, and my life also began at that time when I finally started to dance with life.

What did my childhood teach me about life? That I am lucky I was born into a loving and caring family where plenty of love is shared, not just the love of a parent to her child, but the love from a whole family.

What can I share with you from my story? That having a tough and hard life only teaches us a lesson and creates a solid ground for a great life that is waiting for us to claim. The pressure of life is sometimes necessary to bring a shine and spark into our lives.

> **"A diamond does not start out polished and shining. It once was nothing special, but with enough pressure and time, becomes spectacular."**
>
> –Solange Nicole

I'm that diamond.

"When you've hit rock bottom before and survived, there are very few things in life that can scare you."

~ Unknown

CHAPTER TEN

The Power of Belief

By Jennifer Pompei

I honestly thought I was going to die. I had never felt so much pain in my entire life; and the scary part is, I didn't even know what was happening. There was the most painful thumping in my head and all I remember is telling my husband to call an ambulance, I'm going to die.

The Day Before My World Crashed to Pieces

July 4th, 2002 was a sunny, hot and humid day in Baltimore, Maryland. My boys were four and six years old at the time, and we decided to celebrate the Fourth of July holiday and spend quality family time at the Harbor. We spent the morning touring the various shops and sites as the warm summer breeze blew in off the Chesapeake Bay. It was refreshing, as the temperature continued to rise as the day went on. After lunch we went back to our hotel to cool off and enjoy time in the rooftop pool. As anyone would have guessed, the pool was very crowed, and very warm (bathwater warm). We all love to swim and, as non-refreshing as the warm water was, it was still wet and better than being out in the hot sun. My boys played for hours in the pool (as they always do!), laughing and having fun, and soon it was time to go to dinner and watch the fireworks. That evening as we walked to dinner, I noticed the feeling of water in my ear that I just couldn't get out. Thinking nothing of the water in my ear, the evening festivities continued. After dinner we headed back to the rooftop of our hotel to watch the spectacular fireworks over Inner Harbor. With our boys sitting in our laps, smiling as the colors of the fireworks sparked in their eyes, I smiled with the satisfaction that it had been a wonderful day together.

The next morning, I awoke and prepared for what I anticipated would be another great day. While getting ready, the strangest thing happened: the bathroom started to spin. For the first time in my life, I had gotten dizzy. Not knowing what was happening, I called to my husband Michael who rushed to my side, then led me to the bed so I could lie down. I'm not one for taking it easy and I often say to my family and friends "Suck it up"; however this was something I'd never experienced before. We decided I should take it easy for a couple hours, so I laid down while Michael took the boys to the Science Museum and lunch. Later in the day, I still wasn't feeling any better and nausea had set in, so Michael called our doctor who advised ear drops to help get the water out. After a quick run to the nearest pharmacy, we put the ear drops in and hoped for the best. Day two of our mini vacation was ending, with not near the feelings that day one had provided. The next morning there was no improvement, and my condition had gotten worse. Now, along with the dizziness and nausea, I began to have significant sensitivity to light. Sensing this was more than a simple case of water in the ear, we decided to pack up and head home, which was an hour and a half away. We left Baltimore, and all I remember is lying down for the entire trip with a blanket covering my head, as the sunlight streaming through the windows was unbearable. After dropping our boys off at my parents' house, we went directly to the Emergency Room. While there, I was diagnosed with an inner ear infection causing vertigo, handed some medication and sent home. While receiving this diagnosis did ease my mind briefly, as the day turned to night, my condition didn't improve and by the next morning had worsened. I remember thinking I was going to die from the immense pain in my head. It was a pain unlike anything I had felt in my life. I needed to go back to the hospital, so Michael called for an ambulance. I was in the ER for hours being poked, prodded and examined until they decided to admit me, simply because they didn't know what was wrong but could see I was in a bad way. Over the next several days, many tests were run to try to figure out why I was having so much pain in my head, couldn't walk and couldn't tolerate any light. Test after test, result after result, and several days later, my condition was still perplexing the doctors. I recall late in the day (which is unusual for a doctor to stop in on a patient), one of the doctors, sounding exasperated, said he would like to rule out meningitis; so they performed the first of three spinal taps. Much to their (and my) surprise, they discovered that I had aseptic meningitis. For the next several weeks, I was confined to my hospital room, much of the time with the shades pulled tight and hooked up to a heavy dose of intravenous antibiotics, all with the hope of beating this infection. Many of my memories of this time are vague, but there are some things I remember quite vividly during my hospital stay, such as curling up in the fetal position in the tightest ball and being told not to move for my spinal taps. I remember having a private room and it being very dark with sheets over the windows and my eyes covered most of the time. I remember my vision being very blurred and unable to see, thinking I may lose my eyesight. I remember family visiting, staying with me and being visited by a priest. 27 days is a long time to be stuck in bed, in the hospital. By the time I was discharged, even though the infection had cleared, I was a shell of myself. I was no longer the happy, active mom and wife I had been just one month prior.

Dark Days

Prior to getting the meningitis, I was very active. I was an athlete growing up, and in high school I played softball and was in the marching band. That lifestyle followed me to college, always working out and enjoying life. Soon after graduation, I married my high school sweetheart, got a good job and had two beautiful sons. I was 32, in the prime of my life, and had everything I had ever wanted; in my eyes, it was the perfect life. I worked full-time, worked out, played with my boys, took them to their activities and enjoyed all of it. After the meningitis, I couldn't do anything. The infection caused damage to my inner ear, which made walking and playing with my boys, or anyone, impossible. Being bedridden for 27 days had wrecked my body and my spirit. Behind my smile I was depressed, hopeless, lost, and felt sorry for myself. What had I done to deserve this, and why was this happening to me and my family? I was afraid that for the rest of my life, I wouldn't be able to be active, play with my boys, attend their activities or even dance with them on their wedding days. My mind, body and spirit had all been broken, and it was the darkest time of my life. I was ready to accept that life as I had known it was over.

Recovery or Bust

As I sat in the Vestibular Rehabilitation room for my first therapy visit, I looked down at the worn, tiled floor thinking to myself 'this is a waste of time'. I couldn't look my therapist in the eyes because I was unable to raise my head. If I lifted my head, I'd spin, get dizzy and nauseous. I'd like to think that part of me hoped that the therapy would work, because there was nowhere else to go from the darkness I was in. My therapist explained the damage that was caused in my inner ear and how the inner ear affects many basic functions including balance, walking, head movements, even lying down and sleeping. Normal, everyday functions we all do without thought, I couldn't do. She explained Vestibular Rehabilitation is a special physical therapy program designed to improve balance and reduce problems related to dizziness. We started with an assessment to get a baseline of my abilities, and it wasn't good. I was unable to raise my head from looking at the floor, I was unable to walk a straight line, lie flat, or even read without getting sick. I was diagnosed with Benign Paroxysmal Positional Vertigo (BPPV), which is dizziness generally thought to be due to debris/crystals collected within part of the inner ear (this can be due to an injury or infection). I started going to my Vestibular Rehab three days a week and, because I couldn't drive, needed the assistance of family and friends to take me to these appointments.

We started out slowly, using a CPC Machine (Computer Dynamic Posturography). It is a non-invasive, specialized clinical assessment technique used to quantify the central nervous system mechanisms (central, sensory and motor involved in the control of posture and balance). A vest with parachute straps was placed on me and attached to the machine. When the assessment begins, the floor of the machine moves to simulate moving in a natural environment – but with the safely of the straps in case I would fall, which, I immediately did. Another exercise I did at therapy was walking a straight line. It was such a simple task that I have done forever, but I could no longer do. Who would think that walking a straight line could be this difficult? I was given home exercises to do that worked on my eyes and how they reacted to moving my head. As the weeks of therapy turned into months, I slowly started to see improvements in my balance, walking and raising of my head. My therapist believed in me from day one and said with hard work and being positive I could do anything I wanted, including healing my body and mind. Day after day, month after month, my therapist poured belief and positivity into me. Even if I didn't believe it when I started therapy, her positivity slowly crept into every part of my mind and body. I worked hard at therapy, did my home exercises and started to believe and have faith in myself that I could overcome all the challenges I faced. By the time therapy had ended, I was able to lift my head up without spinning or getting dizzy, I could walk a straight line and beat the CPC Machine – blind folded. The CPC Machine was the ultimate test of my inner balance, as I was unable to use my eyes to compensate and make my inner ear work. I was blind folded as the floor of the machine moved, and I was able to compensate my balance and not fall. I felt accomplished and invincible. The hard work I had put in over eight long months had brought me back to where I was prior to the meningitis. Fifteen years later, I have a few lingering symptoms, such as BPPV, but have learned how to manage them. On my last day of therapy, my therapist sat me down and gave me a framed picture of this quote:

The Greater Part of our happiness or misery depends on our disposition and not our circumstance – Martha Washington

She told me that this quote reflected my belief during my journey to heal. I could've easily given up, but every day at therapy I made the decision to work hard and believe in myself. That belief grew stronger and stronger each session because of her belief in me. I never thought, prior to my illness, about mindset and how it had an impact on my life. She told me that my disposition and attitude during my therapy evolved from being hopeless to hopeful and once I started to believe in myself, I became unstoppable. This is my favorite quote, and the framed picture she gave me fifteen years ago still sits on my desk. I see it every day and I believe that we all have a choice in how our life plays out. You have the choice every second of every day to be happy, sad, loving, angry, grateful or resentful. You choose everyday through your words and actions how you want to live your life, good or bad. Don't forget those around you when you are going down the rabbit hole – negativity attracts negativity. Positivity is contagious; when you start being positive, those around you will catch it too.

Now – Road to Wellness – Healthy

After I recovered from meningitis, I tried to begin living life to the fullest, once again, with my family. While my husband and I had good jobs, were active with our boys, went on nice vacations and lived in our dream home, I was not really looking out for myself. Looking back at the rest of my 30's, I noticed years of overeating, which began a trend of self-loathing. I don't know for sure if my meningitis was an excuse for me to eat whatever I wanted, but for years after it, I struggled with my weight and self-confidence, growing to the largest me in my life. Looking back at family vacations, you are lucky if you find me in any pictures (usually I would be hiding behind my boys). I hated everything about myself, especially how I looked and felt. I was exhausted all the time and would nap almost every day after work. I was also very cranky and negative. I tried every diet, workout plan, pill and piece of equipment I could buy from late night television and nothing seemed to work for me. I'd lose some weight, then I'd gain it back, or sometimes, I wouldn't lose anything. I felt hopeless, defeated, ashamed and frustrated. I was 45 years old and I didn't want to feel like this for the rest of my life. In September 2015, a good friend introduced me to an amazing nutrition system that finally worked for me. Within the first month, I lost some of the extra pounds I had been carrying around for years (dare I say baby weight, 20 years after my boys were born!?) I had boundless energy and slept better than I had in years. I wanted to tell everyone about my nutrition system, but my self-doubt was still there, as the thought of gaining the weight back like I had done so many times before, was front and center in my mind. I kept my weight loss journey to myself for eight months; and even when people asked how I had lost the weight, I told them I was watching what I was eating and exercising. I finally realized I was being selfish by not sharing my wonderful nutrition system and began sharing with friends and family. This brought a new, positive feeling, a sense of purpose, that I could be healthy, happy and help others gain control of their health, love themselves again and feel better than they ever have. I have been using my nutrition system for two and a half years now, have kept the weight off and have never felt better. In addition to my nutrition system I now workout four-five days a week, which is less than prior to losing the weight when I was killing myself with daily workouts! I can honestly say that I love working out now. Finding the right workouts and people were the key to finding my love of fitness. Now, each of these people are part of my tribe and inspire me every day with their amazing attitudes and willingness to help each other. For years, I worked out alone and at home, probably because of how I looked (perceived) and felt (actual). I know that sounds silly now, but the image I had of myself was so low, my mind believed it. As I lost the weight, my self-confidence grew, and I started to try new workouts outside of the house. The key is to find something you enjoy doing, whether it be in-home workouts, classes at a gym, walking in your neighborhood, or trying new workouts and activities to find what you like. Trust me, when you find something you enjoy doing, it no longer become a chore; rather, it is something you love and look forward to doing for the rest of your life.

With my weight finally under control and my self-confidence starting to climb, somehow, I still felt that something was missing. I needed my life to come full circle, I needed to believe in myself the way others saw me. I spent the past year focused on doing much inner work. Yes, I finally found peace within and my purpose.

What you focus on what you find, what you focus on grows, what you focus on seems real, what you focus on you become. – Rod Hairston

I attended an amazing retreat in Hilton Head this past fall, which was led by many inspiring people. I met wonderful people from all over the world that touched my soul and opened my mind and heart. We spent five days practicing gratitude, finding our inner leader, journaling, facing our fears, practicing yoga, taking long walks on the beach, and sharing and learning from one another. I was cracked open at this retreat and saw the full potential of myself. God made me for an incredible purpose, it's time I start using it! I started to focus on the positive things in my life and around it. I became grateful for everything: my faith, health, job, friends, and most of all, my family. If I had a negative thought enter my head (and yes, I did), I'd push it out and think of positive things. Doing this everyday changed how I thought and how I saw the world around me. By following the Law of Focus, it changed my mindset and internal wiring; what you focus on you become. I had become the positive person I wanted to be and spreading that positivity to others has helped me to see the ripple effect of love and light coming back into my life and into the lives of others. To create the life of your dreams, you must love yourself. Focus on your joy and what makes you happy. Do things that make you feel good, and most importantly, love yourself inside and out. Part of changing my mindset has been practicing daily gratitude and journaling about it. Gratitude helps us to see what *is* there instead of what *isn't*. For the first time, I decided to appreciate everything in my life; my husband, my family and friends, and my health. I am abundantly grateful for God's grace and love on this journey called life. At the retreat, I learned the practice of deep breathing. I thought this was a bit silly when I was first introduced to it, but everyone that had been doing it daily swore to its benefits. I quickly fell in love with the peace, calmness and sense of focus it has provided me. We were taught that by focusing on our breathing, we are experiencing the present moment now, the living essence of life. It has also helped me reconnect with God on a deeper level by opening my heart and soul so that I could accept all of His gifts.

Road Ahead

You never know where your life is going to lead you. You think and plan for it to go a certain way and it stops you in your tracks and says, "Hold up, I have something for you to take care of first." Call it a bump in the road or a mountain to climb, it was put there for a reason, even if we don't know why at the time. I truly believe everything happens for a reason and to prepare you for what is next to come in life...and that's what happened to me this past September.

I noticed a small lump behind my right ear, and by December my jaw was aching, I had seen my doctor, and we were monitoring the issue. But by early January my ear was numb, so I asked my doctor for additional testing because I knew that something was wrong. After all, I had spent the past several years finding myself, both physically and emotionally, and had become so in tune with my body that everything was in sync, and I had a feeling – deep down inside - that I needed to get this checked out. Biggest life lesson learned: Be your own self-advocate - listen to and know your body. If something doesn't feel right, advocate until you get an answer that you are comfortable with.

In January 2018, I had an ultrasound that saw an enlarged lymph node behind my right ear, but the ultrasound also found a mass in my Parotid Gland. At this point, I had never heard of the Parotid Gland, so my internet research began! The Parotid Gland is a major salivary gland present on either side of the mouth and in front of both ears. They are the largest of the salivary glands. It secretes saliva through the parotid duct into the mouth, to help chewing and swallowing and to begin the digestion of starches. I had a biopsy of the mass in early February 2018 and received my cancer diagnosis a week later, February 9th – a day I will never forget. To say I was in shock when I received my cancer diagnosis is an understatement.

I went into my appointment thinking it would be a benign mass, no biggie! As I listened to the doctor tell me that they found cancer, I started processing everything in my head, planning and thinking, 'I got this!' All the while, my husband was still in the waiting room, as I didn't think I needed him back there since the diagnosis wasn't going to be cancer. This may sound silly, but one of my first thoughts was that we had lost Savannah, as we were planning on going there to see our youngest son at college over St. Patrick's Day weekend. Yes, I was thinking about our trip and not the cancer. My thought was, 'I'll get the cancer cut out of me and life will go on.' That was until I told my husband about my diagnosis as we crossed the cold, snow-covered parking lot at Hershey Medical Center, at which point it became very real and very scary. I cried but tried to compose myself because I'm not a crier (except for Disney movies!). All I could think about was my family and dying. The fear was there – it crept in fast and hard. Fear is sneaky and shady and tries to get you at your weakest moments, and it did – big time. Yes, I cried at the thought of my boys growing up without me, not walking the beaches of Hilton Head hand in hand with my husband once we retire and many other things. This feeling was short-lived. I pushed it right out of my mind, because I knew deep down to my core I was (and am!) going to beat this with God by my side and the support of my family and friends. I received good news from my PET scan that there was no other cancer found in my body. During the following weeks that led up to my surgery, I continued to focus on filling my body with my amazing nutrition and being physically active. Regardless of my diagnosis, life continued to go on. I still worked out with my friends, as I knew once I had my surgery, I'd have to take some time off and give my body time to heal.

This past year I've been working on having a healthy mindset. Having a positive mindset has been my biggest asset in this battle. It's not wearing rose-colored glasses, but a true sense of positivity on this journey that anything thrown my way I can handle. I have continued to do my deep breathing exercises - deep breathing can be healing to our bodies by flooding our organs with much needed oxygen. Practicing my deep breathing has helped me focus and visualize a body that is strong, healthy, invincible and cancer-free.

I recently had the surgery to remove the cancer in my parotid gland and some surrounding lymph nodes and will begin a series of radiation treatments soon. My recovery has gone well, especially with the support of my family and friends. They have lifted my body and spirit on this journey and have helped me heal from the inside out with their prayers and positivity.

I wouldn't be where I am today without the love and never-ending support of my two sons and husband. Michael has been at my side since we were in high school and has stood with me through the good times and bad. My family is my life, and with their support, I am ready to face any challenges that come my way.

Whether you believe in God, the Universe or a Higher being, I can say that my God has been with me every step of this journey, holding me safely in the palm of His hand, and I know that I am made for a greater purpose.

I recently received a book from a friend, *100 Days to Brave*, and this passage sums up my battle perfectly:

"Being brave isn't something that happens when you're not scared anymore. Brave people don't stop hearing the whispers of fear. They hear the whispers but take action anyway. Being brave is hearing that voice of fear in your head, but saying, "Okay, but the truth is, God made me on purpose and for a purpose." *100 Days to Brave – Annie F. Downs*

Do I still hear the whispers of fear? Absolutely. Do they still scare me? Absolutely. But I know that I am brave, and that gives me purpose to help others on their journeys. If you feel like you are alone – you are not. Look around, because there is always someone holding out a hand to lend you support. Being brave sometimes means asking for support. Tomorrow is a new day and always a blessing. What would you do if there was no tomorrow? Would you mend that broken relationship? Would you love more deeply? Would you take that trip? Would you cherish every moment of every day that you would otherwise take for granted? We don't know what the future has in store, so it is time to start living our lives with a purpose and live like there is no tomorrow.

Downs, Annie F. *100 Days to Brave: Devotions for Unlocking Your Most Courageous Self.* Zondervan, 2017.

"When we hit
our lowest point,
we are open to
the greatest change."

~ Aang, The Legend of Korra

Author Autobiographies

Chapter One

John Spender

John Spender didn't learn how to read and write at a basic level until he was 10 years old. He has since traveled the world started many business's leading him to create the award winning book series 'A Journey Of Riches', he is an Award Winning International Speaker and Movie Maker.

John was an international NLP trainer and has coached thousands of people from various backgrounds through all sorts of challenges. From the borderline home-less to very wealthy individuals, he has helped many people to get in touch with their truth to create a life on their terms.

John's search for answers to living a fulfilling life has take him to working with Native American Indians in the Hills of San Diego, the forests of Madagascar, swimming with humpback whales in Tonga, exploring the Okavango Delta of Botswana and the Great Wall of China. He's travelled from Chile to Slovakia, Hungary to the Solomon Islands, the mountains of Italy and the streets of Mexico.

Every where his journey has taken him, John has discovered a hunger among people to find a new way to live, with a yearning for freedom.

He also co-wrote the script for the film *Adversity* and interviewed all the guests.

Chapter Two

Jen Valadez

Jen is an experienced Emotional Intuitive and Reiki Master, as well as a Licensed Massage Therapist, Vibrational Sound Therapist, Certified Yoga Instructor and a Professional Hiking Guide. She lives in the beautiful red cliffs of Southern Utah and loves being outside and connected to nature.

Jen is passionate about helping others feel their absolute best within their physical body and inspiring them to live their most fulfilled life. Jen has the unique ability of "tapping in" to ones emotional body and identifying areas of repetitive patterns that are keeping them from progressing. She works with clients throughout the world to identify, release, and replace negative trapped emotions and gives them the tools they need to heal their physical, emotional, and energetic body.

Jen has recently created a workshop and travels the U.S. to share her passion for healing, and helps others learn how to connect to the power and spirit which lies within.

You can connect with Jen Valadez at:

yogajen77@gmail.com

jen@livdeephealing.com

www.livdeephealing.com

www.facebook.com/jen.m.valadez

Chapter Three

Ryan Roth

Having called London, Paris, Sydney, Bangkok and Tokyo home, Ryan has experienced more than most.

While owning an art gallery, a branding agency, heading an architecture firm with 400 architects in three countries, a DJ/band management group and most recently the founder of TEDxCanggu and Kabu & Co.

Ryan's been called one of the top 500 cultural influencers in the world, advised three cities in Asia on how to redesign their cities for better living standards and been on a panel discussion where he's faced up to the head of US grain & Monsanto where placed responsibility for 500,000 Indian suicides in the hands of Monsanto and had to give a public lecture to the head of US grain the differences of developed and developing nations.

He's not one to shy away from a public debate and signed to "The London Speakers Bureau". He also loves snowboarding, kiteboarding, loves taxation and will solve global poverty.

links - www.lovelifelivin.com - www.ka-bu.com - <u>instagram.com/bodiroth</u>

Chapter Four

Nicole Doherty

Nicole is a mother, a wife, counsellor and trainer/assessor an entrepreneur and industry leader in the disability & mental health sectors.

She is the CEO/Director of three companies, Wyngate Care which is a Disability, Aged Care, Mental Health Direct Care Service with 30+ staff working in the community, D&M Connect which is a Community Services consulting firm for the vocational education sector, and new company Empowered Liveability which provides Specialist Disability Accommodation building high care housing for people with a disability to promote independence, dignity, respect and above all empower people of all abilities to live life on their terms.

For more information about Nicole www.nicolemdoherty.com

Chapter Five

Tom Baron

Tom was born and raised in south east Michigan. One of three children, Tom is the youngest of his siblings. Although Tom has moved away he is still strongly influenced and committed to his sisters and his family. They are a close knit unit, one which has instilled family values and commitment and pride intertwining in his belief system to this day.

Although Tom has undoubtedly suffered heartache in life, he has chosen to rise above and continues to strive for bettering himself and that of his own family. He now knows that these trials and tribulations have become the vine which led him down his journey to discovering who he truly is and how staying true to his foundational beliefs is one of his best assets.

– In his journey, he has found many riches in "the lessons" and has realized he is right where he needs to be. He is grateful for the amazing connections along the way, to which he has discovered abundant gratitude.

Chapter Six

Suzie Martin Huening

Suzie is a mother of two boys, military spouse, fitness professional, entrepreneur, health coach, and artist. She is licensed Physical Therapist Assistant but currently does't work in the field.

She is a former model and was in several commercials, two movies and a music video. She is passionate about art, and pursing optimal health. She earned her BA in Fine Art with a concentration in Graphic Design.

Suzie used to work for designers doing hand painted furniture, and one of her pieces featured in Family Circle Magazine. She also has been in fitness magazines such as Flex Magazine, Iron Man and Muscle and Fitness from back in her bodybuilding days. Suzie earned her Figure Pro Card as Ms Figure Universe in 2017, a little over a month before her 53rd birthday.

She is proactively seeking to master midlife and inspire others to do the same through exercise, nutrition and mindset.

Chapter Seven

Christian Doherty

Christian, is a vocational education trainer in the community services sector, training mental health, drug and alcohol work and community services to people wanting to work in the field.

He juggles teaching with; being a dad, working out and training Muay Thai, counselling, healing work, and consulting to the mental health and disability sectors.

Christian has a love for consciousness development, particularly psychology and spirituality and spends his spare time absorbing everything he can and being a constant student.

http://www.christianldoherty.com/

Chapter Eight

Kate Williams

Kate is an ambassador for self-love.

Driven to lead others to live an abundant life in harmony with their highest values, Kate is passionate about empowering people to break free of any stigmas holding them back from their dreams.

Attracted into being both a Wellness coach and Hairdresser through her love of helping others, her soul feeds off the deep connection these industries give her – something that is generally lacking in today's digital age.

With a love of both writing and photography, Kate soon hopes to inspire others to dream bigger and live larger through her social pages where she'll be capturing and sharing the discoveries, challenges and triumphs in health, relationships, mindset, and life in general as she embarks on some epic travels of the Australian countryside with her husband and their three extraordinary boys in their home on wheels.

https://www.facebook.com/Katelswilliams

katelswilliams83@gmail.com

Chapter Nine

Putu Cita

Putu Cita was born and grew up on the tropical island of Bali, a tiny island part of the archipelago of Indonesia, in South East Asia.

She grew up in a simple farmer family, Putu has developed her skills in business since the age of 13 years old, when she made her first income from selling fruits and vegetables.

Since then, she has collected numerous experiences working in several types of businesses and at the same time managing her own small ladies apparel. Her great passion and deep caring for human interaction, lead Putu to become an active member of the oldest local non for profit organization in Bali, helping women and children in underprivileged areas of Bali.

Now Putu enjoys her time learning and studying about personal development, with the goal of becoming a successful life coach.

"Life with purpose" is what Putu has always been taught by her late uncle since she was eight years old.

Chapter Ten

Jennifer Pompei

Jennifer is from Harrisburg Pennsylvania and has been married to her high school sweetheart, Michael, for 24 years. They've raised two amazing sons, Anthony 22 and Alex 20, who are both currently in college. Upon receiving her bachelor's degree in environmental science from East Stroudsburg University, Jennifer pursued several exciting opportunities in that field. With a longing to have children, Jennifer left the environmental industry and took a position in health insurance to spend more time with her family.

Having recently become a cancer survivor, Jennifer is now on a personal journey of growth and development and is finding ways to share her positive energy with others to help them overcome issues they may be dealing with. She specializes in healthy living, inside and out, meditation, self-reflection and positive commitments to everything.

Jennifer loves being active, whether with her fitness crew or her family, including their two excitable boxers. Favorite activities include spin class, hiking, biking and kayaking.

www.facebook.com/jennifer.pompei

Afterword

I hope you enjoyed the collection of heart felt stories, wisdom and vulnerability shared. Story telling is the oldest form of communication and I hope you feel inspired to take a step to living a fulfilling life. Feel free to contact any of the authors in this book or the other books in this series.

Please help us get the inspiring messages out to people by leaving an honest review on amazon.com and lets have more people living from the mindset that you can truly do anything with this life.

Other books in the series are...

Transformation Calling: A Journey Of Riches, Book Nine
https://www.amazon.com/Transformation-Calling-Journey-John-Spender-ebook/dp/B07BWQY9FB/

Letting Go and Embracing the New: A Journey Of Riches, Book Eight
https://www.amazon.com/Letting-Go-Embracing-New-Journey/dp/0648284506/

Making Empowering Choices: A Journey Of Riches, Book Seven
https://www.amazon.com/Making-Empowering-Choices-Journey-Riches-ebook/dp/B078JXMK5V

The Benefit of Challenge: A Journey Of Riches, Book Six
 https://www.amazon.com/Benefit-Challenge-Journey-Riches-ebook/dp/B0778S2VBD/

Personal Changes: A Journey Of Riches, Book Five

https://www.amazon.com/Personal-Changes-Journey-John-Spender-ebook/dp/B075WCQM4N/

Dealing with Changes in Life: A Journey Of Riches, Book Four
https://www.amazon.com/Dealing-Changes-Life-Motivational-Inspirational-ebook/dp/B0716RDKK7/

Making Changes: A Journey Of Riches, Book Three
https://www.amazon.com/Making-Changes-Journey-changes-Spiritual-ebook/dp/B01MYWNI5A/

The Gift In Challenge: A Journey Of Riches, Book Two
https://www.amazon.com/Gift-Challenge-Self-Help-Anthology-Spiritual-ebook/dp/B01GBEML4G/

From Darkness into the Light: A Journey Of Riches, Book One
https://www.amazon.com/Darkness-into-Light-Motivation-Inspiration-ebook/dp/B018QMPHJW/

Thank you to all the authors that have shared aspects of their lives in the hope that it will inspire others to live a bigger version of themselves. I heard a great saying from Jim Rohan "You can't complain and feel grateful at the same time" at any given moment we have a chose to either feel like a victim of life or connected and grateful for life. I hope this book helps you to go after your dreams.

www.ingramcontent.com/pod-product-compliance
Lightning Source LLC
Chambersburg PA
CBHW070556100426
42744CB00006B/305